Eduardo Matos Moctezuma

TEOTIHUACÁN

THE CITY OF GODS

RIZZOLI
NEW YORK

First published in the United States of America in 1990 by
RIZZOLI INTERNATIONAL PUBLICATIONS, INC.
300 Park Avenue South, New York, NY 10010

Copyright © 1990
Editoriale Jaca Book spa, Milan, Italy

Original title
Teotihuacan
La metropoli degli dei

Translated from the Italian by
Andrew Ellis

Library of Congress Cataloging-in-Publication Data

Matos Moctezuma, Eduardo.
    Teotihuacán / Eduardo Matos Moctezuma.
        p.   cm.
    ISBN 0-8478-1198-0
    1. Teotihuacán Site (San Juan Teotihuacán, Mexico)   I. Title.
F1219. 1. T27M38   1990   89-43584
972' .52--dc20   CIP

Printed and bound in Italy
by G. Canale & C., Spa, Turin

Table of Contents

Introduction

In the Náhuatl language, the word Teotihuacán means "the place where the gods are created." No name could be more appropriate for a place whose awe-inspiring dimensions prompted the Aztecs (who first discovered the ruins) to transform the city into a myth. Before its fall in A.D. 750, Teotihuacán was the first large town in Central Mexico, with a population of over 100,000 souls and the problems typical of a complex city that had gradually developed over many centuries. The influence of Teotihuacán was felt in distant lands, as far away even as Kaminaljuyú in Guatemala. Owing to its mysterious disappearance, Teotihuacán was hailed as the "City of the Gods" and incorporated into the myths of later races. Thus, Teotihuacán was said to be the birthplace of the Fifth Sun, which brought light to men (who had been created by the god Quetzalcoatl). According to Nahua myths, the past was divided into four Ages or Suns, each one associated with its own deity. These four gods, named Tezcatlipoca and Quetzalcoatl, were the progeny of the supreme deities Tonacacihuatl (mother) and Tonacatecuhtli (father). Each of the four deities governed a cardinal direction of the Universe. Thus, the red god Tezcatlipoca commanded the East, symbolized by the reed (*acatl*), which represented plant growth and fertility. The South was directed by Huitzilopochtli (or blue Tezcatlipoca), symbolized by the rabbit (*tochtli*); this region was known as Huitztlampa, or the place of sacrifice or thorns. The North was presided over by black Tezcatlipoca, with the symbol of the sacrificial knife (*técpatl*); it was named Mictlampa, the region of the dead and the cold. The West, governed by Quetzalcoatl, with the symbol of the house (*calli*), was called Cihuatlampa, the region of women, the place where the sun came to rest. In Teotihuacán culture, special honor was accorded women who died in childbirth: they were said to accompany the sun on its course through the skies from when it rose to when it set, in Cihuatlampa.

The alternating phases of conflict between these deities were considered the chief cause of the eras of history known as Suns. The Nahua people envisioned a dialectical process in which four Suns had passed, leaving them in a fifth, which, according to the *Anales de Cuauhtitlán*,[1] was fated to end in a series of catastrophic earthquakes. But this elaborate conception of the Nahua universe pivoted on a central idea, the core of the cosmos, the home of Ometeotl, who represented the idea of duality in the person of the Old Fire God, Xiuhtecutli. The tangible form of this universal core was the Templo Mayor in the city of Tenochtitlan. From here, one ascended to the upper regions or Skies, or descended into the Underworld. Hence the enormous ceremonial importance of this building. It was here that the fundamental Nahua myths had unfolded, and from here that the four cardinal ways of the Nahua universe issued forth. The Templo Mayor was the center of the world, the heart of an entire cosmology.

One fundamental Nahua myth recounts how the gods gathered on the site of Teotihuacán to create the Fifth Sun, and how one of them, Nanahuatzin, sick and ailing, was persuaded to cast himself into a fire, but arose again in the form of a Sun. Other myths recall how the Sun that rose in Teotihuacán marked the very era in which the peoples'thrived before the arrival of the Spaniards.

> This Sun, called Four-Movement
> this is the Sun
> in which we now live
> it was announced
> when the Sun fell into the fire,
> into the divine fire
> there in Teotihuacán.
> This was also the Sun
> of our Prince, in Tula,
> the Sun of Quetzalcoatl.[2]

Such were the beliefs of the people of Central Mexico. Teotihuacán ceased to be a man-made creation, and was elevated to the City of Gods.

Still other myths were associated with the sacred city. Many of its characteristics recur in later cultures; hence, long after its fall, it continued to exercise an influence on successive cultures in the Valley of Mexico.

In this book we will be exploring Teotihuacán. Thanks to modern archaeology, the earth is gradually yielding its treasures. The murals, houses, pottery, tools and countless other objects have slowly reemerged, and all assist us in our painstaking reconstruction of the history and features of a city that lay buried for over one thousand years.

Chapter One
HISTORICAL PRECEDENTS

Ever since the year 1000 B.C., the Valley of Mexico has been host to scattered groups of human settlers living off its rich harvests and the plentiful fish and wildfowl inhabiting its lakes. Situated some 7,000 feet above sea level, the valley abounded in wildlife, and the people found pelts and skins for clothing, and animal bones and horn from which they fashioned tools similar to those made from other raw materials such as obsidian and silica. They also produced a great deal of pottery of various kinds. The numerous archaeological sites dotted about Lake Texcoco have yielded much evidence of the settlers' production and lifestyle. Among the sites discovered are Zacatenco, Ticomán, Tlatilco, Cuicuilco, Tlapacoya, and Terremote.

One of the more interesting aspects of these sites is that the material unearthed has revealed a substantial change in the lifestyle of the valley's inhabitants, a change signaled by the adoption of farming as the principle form of sustenance. According to data gathered by Richard MacNeish,[1] the first recorded harvests in the Valley of Tehuacán (Puebla) date back to a few millennia earlier, i.e., to between 7000 and 5000 B.C. In the Valley of Mexico, maize and other major crops seem to have been added to the valley people's diet at a later date, in approximately 2500 B.C., as shown by excavations in Zohapilco,[2] where around 2300 B.C. the first very elementary clay figurines appear. But traces of a more complex society do not emerge until about 1000 B.C., and in 600 B.C. we find the first signs of settlements arranged around an important center of ritual activity.

Traditional archaeology has always considered this phase of Mesoamerican development as the close of the Preclassic or Formative period. To my mind, it constitutes a special phase in its own right, one that heralded the appearance of the first settlements on the Central Plateau. Two of these, Tlapacoya and Cuicuilco, are of particular interest.

Tlapacoya

A great deal of new information on Tlapacoya was uncovered by a series of excavations carried out in 1955 by Román Piña Chan (Chan's discoveries were complemented by the studies of Beatríz Barba).[3] The settlement dates back to

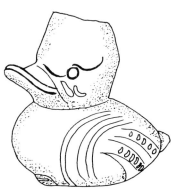

approximately 400 B.C. The digs revealed a stone base that showed signs of having undergone successive later additions, culminating in a four-sided base composed of several sections with stairways at the side, entirely built in stone. Inside the building many significant artifacts were unearthed, among them many pottery items, mostly monochrome, of greatly varied forms. They included bottles, long-necked vases, tripod plates, ollas, and hand-modeled figurines with added details for the eyes and mouths (using *pastillaje* technique).

This stone base at the foot of the Tlapacoya hillside is clear evidence of a more complex social organization and a great advance on the farming villages of earlier times. Tlapacoya was undoubtedly inhabited by a progressive community and acted as the hub of the economic, social, political, and religious activities of the area. Its people controlled the surrounding lands, and were probably in competition with other not-so-distant centers that had germinated around Lake Texcoco.

Some interesting stylistic traits indigenous to Tlapacoya were later fully developed in Teotihuacán, such as certain forms of pottery and particularly architecture.

Cuicuilco

The history of Cuicuilco is of vital importance for understanding what took place before the emergence of Teotihuacán. Like Tlapacoya, Cuicuilco was situated to the south of Lake Texcoco, and greatly influenced the area's destiny. It was destroyed and subsequently abandoned when a small nearby volcano, Xitle, erupted in about 200 B.C., its lava engulfing the center completely. Byron Cummings' research projects[4] of 1922 and 1924 brought to light many valuable finds, including the large circular base of the settlement's most important building. Later, in 1967 and 1968, fresh excavations revealed further building remains.

The large circular base has several sloping sections, all in stone, and apparently once crudely faced with a layer of clay. The upper part of the building was reached

1. 2. 3. From top: goblet with stylized jaguar face; duck-jar; plate with two *Chirostoma* fish native to the freshwater lake. All three engraved ceramic pieces were found in Tlapacoya on the southeast bank of Lake Texcoco, a site dating from 400 B.C. (from Niederberger, 1987).

4. Rectangular stone base with various sections and stairways. Tlapacoya (from Niederberger, 1987).

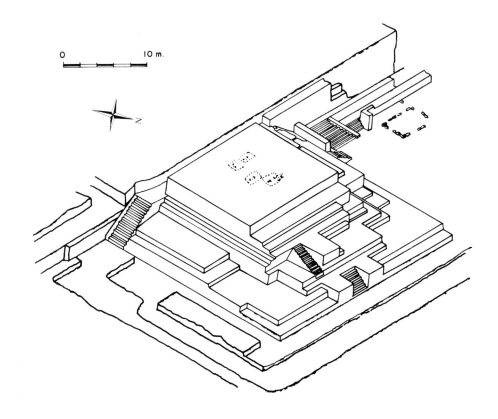

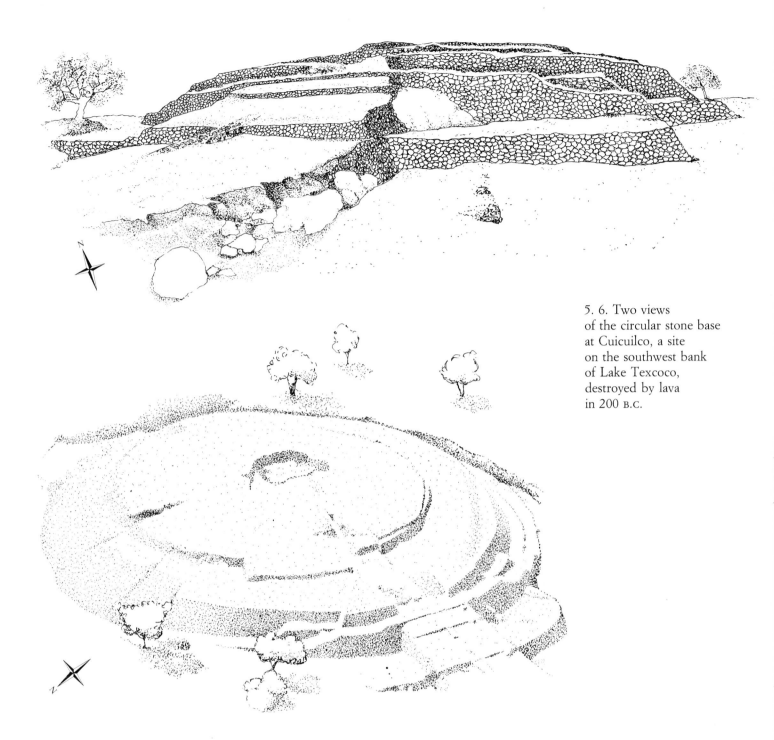

5. 6. Two views
of the circular stone base
at Cuicuilco, a site
on the southwest bank
of Lake Texcoco,
destroyed by lava
in 200 B.C.

by a ramp of steps on the west side, some of which are still visible. The base is approximately 490 feet in diameter, which gives an idea of its original monumental size. The building itself provides a good deal of information on those who built it. In particular, the methods used in transporting the stone and the vast reserves of manpower needed to accomplish this task suggest that an elite class ruled over the community and employed it in the construction of religious monuments. There is little doubt that this building had a religious function. Later excavations revealed other bases made of earth or compressed clay, either square or rectangular, with steps on one side, similar to the first structure.

These finds confirm that Cuicuilco grew into a thriving ceremonial center. The main activity was most likely farming. Recent geological studies have shown that before the eruption of Xitle several rivers flowed through the area, creating a highly fertile catchment. The nearby lake was also a plentiful source of food, providing not only fish but a host of waterfowl and aquatic plants. It is likely that, being a large center of government, Cuicuilco controlled several riverside villages, such as Terremote,[5] where evidence has been found of a group largely devoted to basket weaving, fishing, and hunting.

Besides the ruins of temple bases found in Cuicuilco, which may well predate those of Teotihuacán itself, there have been other interesting finds: for example, a clay statue of the Fire God, resembling the many stone effigies of him found in Teotihuacán. He is portrayed as a cross-legged old man, wrinkled and toothless, leaning forward with a huge brazier on his head. It is hardly surprising that the locals worshipped him, considering that Cuicuilco was destroyed by fire and lava. This cult was observed even in more recent times, and evidence of the Old God (called Huehueteotl by the Aztecs) has turned up in the pantheons of the Teotihuacán, Toltec and Aztec peoples.

After the destruction of Cuicuilco, the surviving population presumably migrated north along the lakeside, and evidence of the worship of the Fire God in Teotihuacán would suggest that the people of Cuicuilco were somehow connected with the foundation of the great city.

Terremote-Tlaltenco

Like many other settlements of this period, Terremote was situated to the south of Lake Texcoco. Excavations made in a mound revealed traces of a settlement. Terremote was probably a fishing village which thrived off the fauna offered by the nearby lake. There are remains of various items, such as rope, nets, and baskets, which were probably directly related to the community's day-to-day activity.

On the basis of the distribution of the various archaeological remains (pottery, stone tools, bones, etc.), various different areas of the mound have been identified. One section was apparently devoted to the production of textiles. In another, the many fragments of receptacles around the hearths suggest an area for food preparation. A third section served as a burial ground. In Terremote a wide range of tools have come to light, including stone *metates* (mortars) and *manos* (pestles), scrapers, rasps, needles, and spatulas.

Analysis of its chronology has led experts to date the settlement between 400 B.C. and A.D. 1, making it practically contemporary with the two other major centers, Cuicuilco and Tlapacoya. While the pottery of these two settlements is more elaborate than that of Terremote (which is not surprising, as Cuicuilco and Tlapacoya were the first ceremonial centers in the Valley of Mexico), there are some similarities in the types produced.

Given the proximity of Terremote to these two powerful centers, whose elite class undoubtedly also controlled the hinterland, it is quite likely that part of its production went into the storerooms of Cuicuilco or Tlapacoya. There is evidence to suggest that, at this stage in the development of the valley, there were diverse vassal groups laboring for the benefit of ruling classes. This kind of organization and control fostered the emergence of a full-fledged state.

The Teotihuacán Valley

Excavations in the Teotihuacán Valley have shed light on the Cuanalan and Tezoyuca phases. The first of these stretches from 500 B.C. to 250 B.C., and the second to around the year 200 B.C. The Tezoyuca phase is particularly important, because five archaeological sites have been discovered whose position indicates they

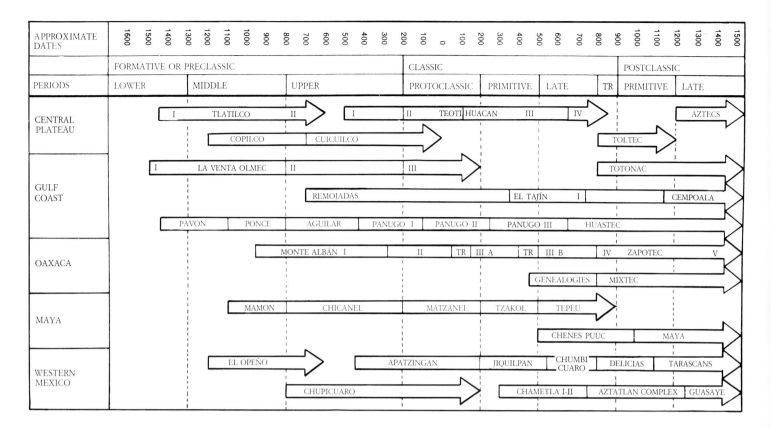

were defense systems. The pottery remains betray the influence of a northern culture, particularly the fragments of Chupícuaro ware and other pieces that seem to emulate the more southerly Cuicuilco tradition. The influence of Cuicuilco and Tlapacoya during this phase was undoubtedly considerable. Certain natural features of the Teotihuacán Valley made it an ideal environment for settlement. When the dominating center Cuicuilco, south of the lake, was destroyed by lava, conditions were ripe for the development of a new civilization, born of centuries of experience. This development would find its ultimate expression in a new settlement, in which the ruling elite, with their calendar and profound knowledge of astronomy, agriculture and war, would achieve levels of social organization advanced enough to engender the largest city in the Central Plateau, Teotihuacán.

7. Chronological table of the ancient civilizations of Mesoamerica (from Piña Chan, 1972).

Chapter Two
THE SEARCH
FOR TEOTIHUACÁN

Over the centuries, a fair number of excavations and studies have been devoted to Teotihuacán. The first to probe beneath the topsoil were the Aztecs, who migrated to the Valley of Mexico many centuries after the fall of Teotihuacán. They did not take long to grasp the unique significance of the mysterious city and, although it was half-hidden beneath a thick mantle of vegetation, they declared it sacred and incorporated it into their mythology. It is hardly surprising that the Aztecs were prompted to dig up the treasures of the sacred city. Otherwise there would be no explanation for the original and imitation Teotihuacán artifacts in the Templo Mayor of the Aztecs capital, Tenochtitlan. Indeed, the indelible link between the two civilizations is corroborated by the similarity of remains found in their cities.

Among the many features linking Teotihuacán with the Aztec capital, which stood on the site of today's Mexico City, was their common urban plan. Both cities were divided into four distinct sections or quadrants by two imposing causeways leading out of the city in each of the four cardinal directions. In the Aztec city, the causeways led to Ixtapalapa and Tepeyac (the north-south axis), and the grand east-west causeway cut through the city behind the Templo Mayor and led to nearby Tacuba. In Teotihuacán, the north-south causeway is known as the Calle de los Muertos or Avenue of the Dead, while the East-West Avenue bisects the Avenue of the Dead at the Ciudadela. Furthermore, the Templo Mayor of the Aztecs had the same number of *taludes* (sloping apron stones) as the Moon and Sun pyramids of Teotihuacán, though the entire Aztec building was set on a vast platform or plinth. It is also interesting that the Aztec ceremonial area consisted of a platform enclosing various buildings in a sort of sacred precinct. In Teotihuacán, this platform or precinct included the Sun Pyramid and the Ciudadela. The Aztec complex also enclosed secondary shrines such as the set of Templos Rojos (or red temples) all built in the *talud-tablero* design—a sloping apron (*talud*) surmounted by a horizontal, rectangular panel (*tablero*)—typical of Teotihuacán architecture. One of these temples was adorned with the painted designs (*medios ojos* or "half-eyes") that recurred frequently throughout Teotihuacán (principally to portray running water), although those appearing on the Aztec temples were larger and more crudely made. An Aztec sculpture of the Old God Huehueteotl found very close to the north-facing Templo Rojo, retains the typical features of its earlier Teotihuacán counterpart: he is depicted as a seated god bearing a huge brazier on his head. It is fairly certain from its location that the statue was originally sited by the Aztecs high on the altar of the Templo Rojo. Besides these, other Teotihuacán features have emerged in the Aztec Templo Mayor in Tenochtitlan, such as masks and pottery remains, all documented by the experts working on the Proyecto Templo Mayor.[1]

The Sixteenth Century Chroniclers

Various chronicles dating from the sixteenth century invariably refer to Teotihuacán in one of two ways: either as a place with two great temples or hills dedicated to the Sun and Moon (some even recall that each was crowned with a stone statue), or as a mythical city of ancient times.

Some sources relate that Teotihuacán was inhabited by giants; in fact the city, which by A.D. 750 was completely deserted, inspired a great many strange tales, some recounted by the Aztecs themselves, others reported by the Spanish chroniclers.

The first such story we will look at is the version related by one of the main Spanish chroniclers, a friar, Bernardino de Sahagún:

> From Tamoanchán they went to carry out sacrifices to the village called Teotihuacán, where in honor of the Sun and the Moon they constructed two hills, and in this village they elected those who would rule over all others, which is why they called the place Teotihuacán, or Ueitiuacán, which means the place where the sovereigns were chosen.
>
> In that place, furthermore, they buried their most important men and leaders, and on their tombs they erected mounds of earth, which can be seen even today, and look like small man-made hills; and one can still see the quarries where they mined their stone, and the rocks from which they built the tumuli. And the tumuli consecrated to the Sun and the Moon are like large mounds made by hand, like natural mounds, but they are not, and it may seem far-fetched to say they were man-made, but they most certainly were, because those who built them were giants. This is obvious from the mound called Cerro Chollullan, which is clearly man-made, because it contains raw brick and ornaments.
>
> And this place was called Teotihuacán, the village of Téotl, a deity, because the superior men who were buried here when they died were likened to gods and did not die, but awoke from the dream in which they had existed; which is why the ancients said that after death people did not perish, but regained their lives, as if awakening from a dream, and were transformed into spirits or gods.[2]

Another friar, Jerónimo de Mendieta, gives a first-hand account of Teotihuacán:

> Close by the village of Teotihuacán there are many temples or *teucales*, complete with plinth or base, and one in particular of outstanding size and height, still crowned by a stone idol (which I have seen) so great that there was no way it could be removed from its place and taken away.[3]

The chronicler Juan de Torquemada notes:

> What I can say about it is that the Indios of this Nueva España had two temples of great height and size—constructed six leagues from this town, near San Juan Teotihuacán—which were outside the inhabited areas, and still are, though not at a great distance, and around them there are over two thousand other [temple] bases; for this reason the place is called Teotihuacán, the Place of the Gods.[4]

In Francisco del Paso y Troncoso's account, *Papeles de la Nueva España*, there are also references to Teotihuacán. He mentions the stone statues at the summit of the pyramids, and tells how even the Aztec sovereign Motecuhzoma himself went on pilgrimage to the place, laden with offerings:

> At the top of it stood an idol of stone which they called Tonacateuctli, fashioned from a single block of hard rock three arms long, one wide, and just as thick; it was set facing west...

Later he adds:

> ...A short way further on, from the north side, there was another *cu* [temple], which they named after the Moon, on the summit of which stood another idol almost three arms high, which they called The Moon; all around there were many other *cues*, and on one of them, the largest, six more idols called Brothers of the Moon, which were visited by the priests of Motecuhzoma, Lord of Mexico, every twenty days for sacrificial purposes: during the year, they celebrated eighteen festivals, every twenty days a festival, each with a different ceremony...[5]

Of all the Nahua myths on Teotihuacán, one is particularly important, as it concerns the birth of the Fifth Sun in the city. The following description by Sahagún is worth quoting at length. It shows why successive peoples venerated Teotihuacán as an integral part of their conception of the cosmos:

> They say that, before day was first come to the world, all the gods came together in a place called Teotihuacán, today the village of San Juan, between Chiconauhtlán and Otumba, and then they questioned one another, saying: "Who will bring light to the world?"
>
> Upon hearing these words, a deity by the name of Tecuciztécatl replied: "I shall take it upon myself to bring light to the world." Once again the gods spoke, saying: "Who shall be the next?" Then they looked one upon the other and asked themselves who should be the second: but they were all fearful and hid themselves.
>
> One among them, whom no one had noticed, who was covered in pustules, did not speak, and listened to what the others were saying, until they turned to him, saying: "It shall be you, afflicted one, who shall bring light to the world." And with good will he obeyed their request, and said: "Gratefully I accept what you have instructed me to do, and so be it."
>
> And so the two of them began a penitence lasting four days, and then lit the flames in the hearth, which was prepared on a rocky mound which we now call *teotexcalli*. Each offering made by the god Tecuciztécatl was something precious. He brought sumptuous plumage called *quetzalli* in place of branches, balls of gold in place of balls of hay, needles of precious stones instead of needles made of *maguey* [Mexican agave], needles of colored coral instead of blood-soaked needles; and likewise precious was the *copal* that he offered up.
>
> And the afflicted one, whose name was Nanahuatzin, instead of branches, offered up green canes bound together in threes and then in bundles of nine; and he offered balls of hay and needles of *maguey*, and he soaked them in his own blood; and instead of *copal* he offered the weals of his own pustules. Each of the two built himself a tower in the form of a mound, and on these mounds they observed a penitence of four nights. These mounds are now called *tzaqualli*, and they are both situated near the village of San Juan, called Teotihuacán.
>
> Once the four nights of penitence were at an end, each left the branches and other instruments of his penitence on his mound.

This they did, once their penitence was at an end, the night in which after midnight they had to prepare themselves to do what had been established; shortly before midnight they prepared the ornaments for the god Tecuciztécatl; they gave him a set of plumes called *aztacómitl*, and a coat of cloth; and on the head of the sick one called Nanahuatzin they placed a hat of paper, called *amatzontli*, and did girt him in a stole of paper and a *maxtli* [loincloth] of paper; and when midnight was come, all the gods gathered about the hearth called *teotexcalli* where the fire burned for four days.

The gods gathered about in two rows around the fire, on either side; and the two gods mentioned above came forth, their faces turned to the flames, between the two rows of gods.

All were standing, and they said unto Tecuciztécatl: "Come, Tecuciztécatl, enter the flames!" And at once Tecuciztécatl readied himself for the flames; but since the fire burned fiercely, and he felt the intense heat of the flames, he withdrew in fear, and dared not cast himself into it.

Once again Tecuciztécatl assayed to cast himself into the flames, summoning his courage, but when he came near he held back and dared not enter; for four times he tried, but dared not. It had been established that he would not make more than four attempts.

When Tecuciztécatl had tried four times, the gods turned to Nanahuatzin and said unto him: "Come, Nanahuatzin, you try!"

And no sooner had the gods thus spoken, than Nanahuatzin summoned his courage. With eyes closed he prepared himself and leaped into the flames: it immediately burned more vigorously and leaped about, as if it were roasting; and when Tecuciztécatl saw that Nanahuatzin had cast himself into the fire and burned, he came forward and he too leaped into the fire.

And it is said that at once an eagle flew into the flames and burned, which is why it has darkened plumage; and at the end, a jaguar also entered the flames, but did not burn entirely, which is why it is thus speckled with black and white.

And for this reason, all the valorous warriors are called *quauhtlocélotl*, and the first in war is called *quauhtli*, because the eagle entered into the fire first, while the second is called *océlotl*, because the jaguar entered the flames after the eagle.

After both gods had cast themselves into the fire and had burned, the others sat around about and awaited to see from what side Nanahuatzin would reemerge. They remained waiting for much time, and in the end, the skies began to change color, and everywhere about the light of dawn began to appear.[6]

As we can see, the Nahua peoples (including the Aztecs) attributed considerable importance to Teotihuacán, as the rising of the Fifth Sun, the guiding light of the world, was directly linked to the city's name.

Early Excavations and Descriptions

The first organized excavations on the pyramids were undertaken around 1675 by the Mexican literary figure, Carlos de Sigüenza y Góngora (1645-1700). Apparently, his research focused largely on the Moon Pyramid, where he opened a tunnel in the front. Unfortunately we know little of the excavations themselves, but archaeologists later found Sigüenza's tunnel, as we shall see. In fact, his excavations are considered the first scientific exploration ever conducted in America.

Sigüenza and his work are thus described by Ignacio Bernal:

It is Sigüenza... who leads the first true archaeological research, which is aimed at studying a monument with the purpose of casting light on historical facts.[7]

Several descriptions of the ancient city date from the end of the seventeenth century, such as those by the Italian traveler Giovanni Francesco Gemelli Carreri in 1700.[8] The opinions expressed by Gemelli Carreri are often attributed to his Mexican literary friend, Sigüenza y Góngora.

In 1767, the Jesuits were suddenly expelled from Nueva España and all territories under the rule of Carlos III of Spain. Many priests of the Compañía de Jésus moved to Italy, including Francesco Saverio Clavigero, who wrote and published a text in Italian.[9] In this work he refers to Teotihuacán and retraces what earlier chroniclers had said about the Sun and Moon pyramids, and the idols at their summit, reporting that the gold once covering them had been stripped off by Spanish conquistadores, and the sculptures destroyed by the first Bishop of Mexico. With regard to the gold, it must be said that Teotihuacán has so far yielded no gold objects, which would seem to contradict Clavigero's account.

The next we hear of Teotihuacán, comes some years later from one Baron Alexander von Humboldt, who arrived in Mexico in 1803, and wrote on its history in his book, *Vue des Cordillères*, in which he describes various archaeological monuments. On Teotihuacán, Humboldt writes:

> The group of pyramids of Teotihuacán stand in the Valley of Mexico, eight leagues northeast of the Capital in a plain called Micoatl or the Avenue of the Dead. Two of the largest pyramids are still standing, those dedicated to the Sun (Tonatiuh) and to the Moon (Meztli), and many other smaller mounds around these, forming streets exactly oriented either north to south or east to west. One of the larger *teocalli* [pyramids] is 180 feet high, the other is approximately 140; the base of Tonatiuh Iztacal is roughly 680 feet in length, according to Oteyza who measured it in 1803, making it even bigger than the Egyptian pyramid of Mycerinus, the third largest of the great pyramids of Giza, and almost equal to the Khafre pyramid in terms of the length of its base. The smaller pyramids, which, according to tradition, served as tombs for the heads of the tribes, were no more than thirty to thirty-five feet high. In Egypt too, the Mycerinus and Cheops pyramids are surrounded by eight smaller ones, symmetrically arranged in front of the higher ones. It is still possible to make out the form of the steps leading up to the two *teocalli* of Teotihuacán, four altogether, subdivided into many smaller ones whose nucleus of mixed clay and stone is clad in a thick wall of *tezontle*, or porous volcanic rock. This construction is similar to one of the pyramids of Saqqara, which has eight sections of descending size, and is a mound of stones and yellow mortar covered with rough stones, according to Pocoke's travelogue. Two colossal statues representing the Sun and the Moon surmount the Mexican *teocalli*, and were hewn from rock and clad in gold, which Cortés' soldiers removed. Bishop Zumaraga, a Franciscan, saw to the destruction of everything relating to the cults, history and antiquity of the indigenous peoples of America, and also ordered the idols from the Micoatl plains to be smashed; there are still remains of a stairway leading up to the platform of the *teocalli*.[10]

Humboldt's comparison between the Teotihuacán pyramids and those in Egypt is fascinating, especially his reference to the pyramid of Saqqara, which is actually very similar in form.

Some years after the uprisings for Mexican independence, which culminated in 1821, new descriptions of the area were published. One important account is that of the Marquise Fanny Calderón de la Barca (the wife of the first Ambassador sent to Mexico by the king of Spain), who has left us a full account of the country.[11] The Marquise visited Teotihuacán and mentions the Sun and Moon pyramids, but mistakenly blames the Spanish for the devastation of the site.

In 1864 new measurements and excavations were made in Teotihuacán by the Comisión Científica de Pachuca, piloted by Ramón Almaraz. The results of this research, published a year later,[12] mention the pyramids. The most important undertaking described involved fixing the geographical coordinates of the two pyramids and the Ciudadela. A complete location map of the site was also made. In his report, Almaraz refers to the platform surrounding the Sun Pyramid, and makes some erroneous calculations regarding the distribution of mounds in the Ciudadela (he says that there were three mounds on the west side when there are in fact four). Almaraz also notes that the mounds were partially destroyed, and mentions having dug into one of them and found walls and steps. He is probably referring to one of the two mounds on the central stretch of the Avenue of the Dead.

In 1885 the French archaeologist, Désiré Charnay,[13] published a book devoted entirely to surveys carried out in sites on the Central Plateau and other nearby areas, including some Maya locations. In Teotihuacán Charnay excavated two separate areas: one in the cemetery of the village of San Juan, the other on a mound west of the Avenue of the Dead, corresponding to the Superimposed Buildings Complex. Charnay also made a photographic survey, a technique that was just becoming standard practice in archaeology.

In 1884-86 Leopoldo Batres undertook his first excavation of Teotihuacán, concentrating his efforts mainly on the last stretch of the Avenue of the Dead (a few yards from the Moon Pyramid), where he worked on a monument now known as the Templo de la Agricultura. The murals unearthed by Batres were evidently an astonishing sight. They depicted a long, detailed series of plants and votive offerings. Sadly, nothing of these murals remains today, though we know what they were like from a set of drawings made at the time. Manuel Gamio was highly critical of Batres' working methods, and more recently Ignacio Bernal had this to say:

> ...this self-taught man explored these places with no knowledge whatever of digging techniques or serious study methods. There is more useful information in the modest excavations of Charnay in Teotihuacán than in all the research Batres carried out in the immense city.[14]

Alfredo Chavero's work was altogether different. Entrusted with the Pre-Hispanic section of the project entitled *México a Través de los Siglos,* Chavero gathered every available scrap of information to support his erroneous theory that Teotihuacán was an example of Toltec culture. Working with data from recent excavations by the Comisión Científica de Pachuca and studies by Gumersindo Mendoza and Antonio García Cubas, Chavero also drew on the photographic surveys completed by Désiré Charnay. As could be expected, he examined the Sun and Moon pyramids, observing that they were built in locally mined volcanic *tezontle* rock. He described the platform around the Sun Pyramid as a form of defense wall, noting the orientation of both monuments and the shaft and tunnels discovered inside the Moon Pyramid. He suggested that these passages might be funeral chambers, and that there might be internal passageways. But what Chavero had stumbled across were probably the excavations made by Sigüenza toward the end of the seventeenth century. Another important feature Chavero focused on was the type of metric unit used by the builders. Note also his fine description of the Ciudadela:

> About eight hundred and seventy yards south of the Sun Pyramid there is an unusual complex called the Ciudadela. Four walls set at right angles form an almost perfect rectangle. They are two hundred and sixty feet in width and have an average height of thirty, except for the eastern wall, which is only sixteen feet

high. On the walls, there are four *tlateles* [mounds] on the south side, another four on the north side, and three each on the other two sides.[15]

From the description that follows, we can see that Chavero believed these mounds of earth were mortuary tumuli (something people had believed since the sixteenth century), although Mendoza (whom Chavero quotes) had suggested the function they are recognized for today:

> Other smaller constructions are connected to the pyramids, including tumuli or *tlateles*. Those that lie around the Sun Pyramid are approximately twenty-nine feet high, and served, tradition has it, as sepulchers for the head tribesmen and lords. The *tlateles* are of varying size: in their interior, gold objects and worked stones have been found, and in one a large idol ten feet in height. While many of them served as sepulchers, Mr. Mendoza believes that the others served as the foundations of temples to minor gods, and in many cases as individual dwellings for the inhabitants of the city; from the remains one can infer that these houses had plastered floors and walls, and plaster was used even in the alleyways between houses; the plaster was usually red in color, as in the case of the pyramids, or of some other color. But as we know, Charnay also unearthed the remains of larger dwellings, making a photographic record of some of them, which he called palaces. Seen from afar, the *tlateles* seem to spread out endlessly in every direction; it has been calculated that, with the Sun Pyramid as the center, they stretch for a league and a half. This seems to confirm the suggestion that besides being the city of the gods, Teotihuacán was also a Toltec necropolis.[16]

In 1877 Gumersindo Mendoza published an article on Teotihuacán,[17] in which he referred to data supplied by the Comisión Científica de Pachuca. Significantly, he recalled the superimposition of structures, and commented on the various levels revealed in the excavations. He felt that the city stretched outward a good "league and half" (four to five miles).

Toward the close of the nineteenth century, further mention of Teotihuacán is made by H. Bancroft[18] and by William Holmes,[19] and later by Zelia Nuttall.[20]

In 1895, García Cubas found the tunnels in the Moon Pyramid mentioned above, which he considered as old as the pyramid itself. During other digs east of the Avenue of the Dead, he came across a set of smooth walls and an additional wall painted in polychrome featuring what he termed a "rare animal" set against a background of "irregular oblique bands painted in light blue, red and green."[21] This description resembles the mural found in 1963-64 in this area, showing a huge jaguar set against diagonal bands of color. It may well have been the same mural.

In 1900 Antonio Peñafiel published his monograph on Teotihuacán.[22] But the most noteworthy discoveries of the first decades of this century were in the new digs made by Leopoldo Batres at various points around the Teotihuacán site. Batres began his exploration work[23] in 1905, in view of the approaching centenary celebration of Mexican Independence, and concentrated his efforts on the Sun Pyramid. His conclusions were bitterly criticized. This is what Manuel Gamio said:

> Once again, [Batres] failed to make a general or detailed site map of the existing mounds in the area. The pyramid was altered; he removed a layer twenty-three feet deep from the south side, and other layers of varying depth from the other sides. The original profile was not protected accordingly, and consequently its shape shows marked signs of decay; it is unimaginable that the original structure was so irregular, given the precision of the craftsmanship and the almost perfect

8. Section of the archaeological area of Teotihuacán in 1905-10, during excavations conducted by Leopoldo Batres: "Fence, Santa María ditch, central mound of Ciudadela [Templo de Quetzalcoatl], San Juan river, pyramid railway cutting, Sun Pyramid, Moon Pyramid, fence" (from Gamio, 1922, Plate 9b).

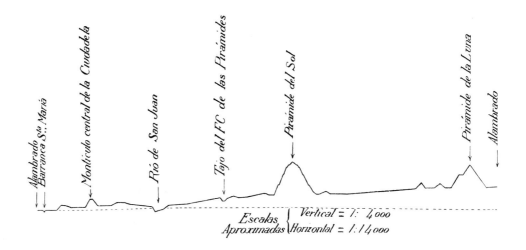

design of other such buildings. As for the construction techniques, Batres' description does not coincide with what has come to light from our excavations, as we shall see later on. Batres did not even trouble to remove the rubble, and left large piles of earth which altered the original topography of the mounds.

The Ferrocarril [railway] de las Pirámides linking the Sun Pyramid with the station of the Ferrocarril Mexicana was built right through the monuments themselves, damaging them in places.[24]

During the various sessions of the International Congress of Americanologists, many reports were devoted to Teotihuacán. One of the first was Wardle Newell's essay "Certain Clay Figures of Teotihuacán,"[25] for the XIII Congress, held in New York in 1902. Another important one was Stansbury Hagar's report[26] (for the 1910 Congress in Mexico City), which Manuel Gamio considered to be based on a somewhat farfetched premise. The 1912 Congress was held in London, and included reports by Madame Barnett on Teotihuacán terracotta heads,[27] Franz Boas[28] on research completed by the Escuela Internacional in the Valley of Mexico, and Eduard Seler[29] on the design similarities between certain Teotihuacán murals and types of Mexican pottery.

In 1915 Seler published his "La Cultura de Teotihuacán,"[30] a monograph lauded by Ignacio Bernal as an authentic cultural inquiry based on the accurate assessment of archaeological data.

In 1917, after deliberations taken by the Congreso de la Unión, an agreement was reached to set up the Departamento de Arqueología y Etnografía within the Mexican Ministry of Agriculture and Economy. In 1919 the department changed its name to the Dirección de Antropología. Its director from 1917 to 1924 was Manuel Gamio, who laid the foundations for a sweeping research program entitled *La Población del Valle de Teotihuacán.*

"La Población del Valle de Teotihuacán" by Manuel Gamio

Gamio's idea of choosing specific areas of each region for study stemmed from the need to design a coherent program capable of embracing the entire country. With this in mind, Gamio initiated a research program run by the Dirección de Antropología which incorporated the following objectives:

1. The gradual acquisition of data on racial characteristics, on all manifestations of material and intellectual culture, on idioms and dialects, on the

economic situation and conditions of the physical and biological environment of the Republic's regional populations of both past and present.

2. An assessment of the commitment required from public bodies (federal, local, and municipal) and private organizations (religious institutions, scientific or worker associations, the Press, the Church, etc.) for furthering the physical, intellectual, moral and economic development of these populations.

3. Preliminaries for racial integration, cultural fusion, linguistic unification and economic integration of these groups, without which the formation of a coherent and fully defined nation, a true mother-country, was not feasible.[31]

To put these objectives into practice, Gamio subdivided the national territory into eleven regions, classifying them according to the kinds of social groups inhabiting them, as well as the climatic, biological and other special aspects of each region. The eleven regions were as follows: 1) Valley of Mexico, Hidalgo, Puebla, and Tlaxcala; 2) Oaxaca and Guerrero; 3) Chiapas; 4) Yucatán and Quintana Roo; 5) Tabasco and Campeche; 6) Veracruz and Tamaulipas; 7) Jalisco and Michoacán; 8) Queretaro and Guanajuato; 9) Chihuahua and Coahuila; 10) Sonora and Sinaloa; 11) Baja California.

Gamio proposed that each year one or two populations typical of each region would be the subject of an in-depth study. The first he chose was the population of the Teotihuacán Valley, as typical of the first region.

In his introduction Gamio explained his basic approach program, and the reason for his decision to analyze the relatively simple features of population and territory:

> Since from nearly all points of view, population and territory are two intimately linked and interdependent entities, it is vital to understand both in great depth so as to improve the material and spiritual conditions of the people's lives.[32]

This approach led to two fundamental considerations. On the one hand, the study would be comprehensive, i.e., from a method point of view it would extend from the Pre-Hispanic populations to those of the present day; and on the other, its object would be to improve all aspects of the living conditions of the people under study. The program was therefore clearly founded on the practical application of a scientific method to a concrete situation. In order to appreciate better the implications of this approach, let us look at some of the methodological features listed by Gamio.

a) DEFINING THE PROBLEM

Gamio suggested a major focal point for research: the study of two large groups—Indios and Mestizo or mixed race—with their various social and cultural differences, revealing the considerable backwardness of the first group compared with the second:

> Actually, our population is by no means homogeneous but quite dissimilar, given that the groups it is composed of have distinct historical legacies, racial characteristics, and material and mental differences; furthermore there is a very broad range of languages and dialects.[33]

Thus Gamio's global program was aimed at achieving a full grasp of the history of the territories and their populations. On the question of the different populations, Gamio wrote:

> In its three development phases of Precolonial, Colonial, and Contemporary, the population of the Teotihuacán Valley presents an inverse or downward

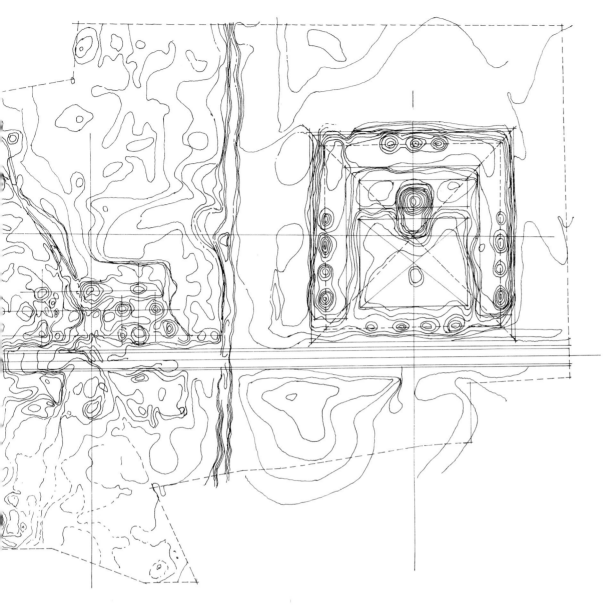

9. Map of Teotihuacán in 1917 before excavations by Manuel Gamio (from Gamio, 1922, Plate 8).

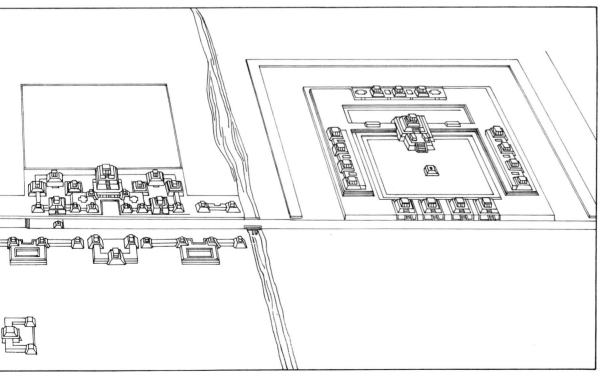

10. Perspective reconstruction of Teotihuacán by Ignacio Marquina (from Gamio, 1922, Plate 12).

11. The Ciudadela before and after excavations by Manuel Gamio (from Gamio, 1922, Plate V).

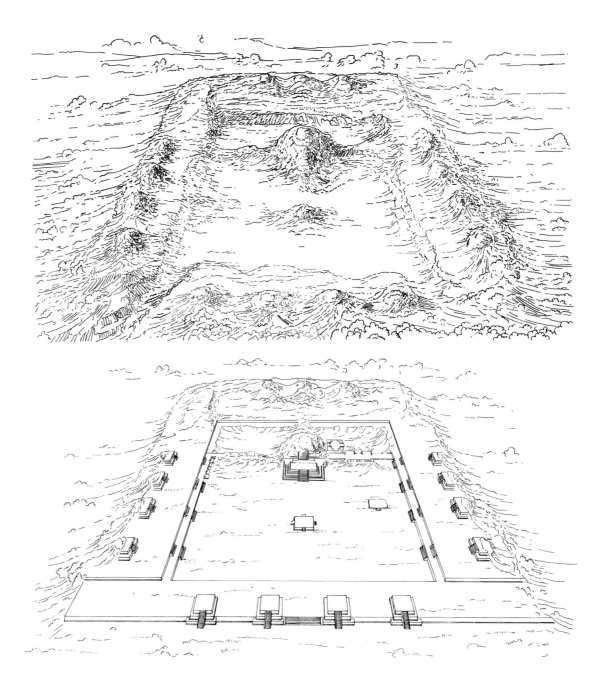

evolution. During the first period, the inhabitants of the region thrived on both intellectual and material levels, as is amply testified by the lively traditions and magnificent relics of all kinds. The Colonial age spelled decline, and the populations lost their nationality, as the alien culture of the Spanish invaders destroyed or swept aside every manifestation of native lore, government, art, industry, religion, uses and customs; the newcomers had nothing to give in exchange, or were unwilling. In the face of such adversity, the races and their farming survived; the only flourishing cultural feature in this Colonial period is the marked indigenous influence on Spanish architecture. During the last period, which spans from the start of the nineteenth century to the present day, the increasing decline of indigenous culture has been alarming, and the inhabitants have lost virtually all they had of their one primary asset—the farm land to which they belonged. As for native rights and self-determination sanctioned by the independence movement of 1810, they are not implemented or are ineffective, almost as if the area was still in the grip of colonialism. What is the cause of this inexorable decline, which threatens to lead to an irreparable collapse? What tools are needed to guarantee the free development of this beleaguered population?[34]

Earlier I pointed out how Gamio's research program provided a useful means for assessing its theoretical premises, basic methods and technique. Manuel Villa Aguilera has shown that Gamio's logic is based on a subtle presupposition, namely, the existence of two groups—Indios and Mestizo—each with its sociocultural identity. The first group lags considerably behind the second. The problem situation thus affecting the nation can be addressed on two different fronts, one theoretical and the other methodological. The first entails focalizing the general aspects of the problem, viewing them as a whole and as a practical issue to be solved. The second considers the global study the key to understanding the social groups and their characteristics, from their distant origins to the present-day reality, in the context of the topics listed earlier. On this subject, Villa Aguilera writes:

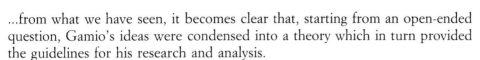

12. Inner core diagram of the Templo de Quetzalcoatl in the Ciudadela (from Gamio, 1922, Fig. 35).

> ...from what we have seen, it becomes clear that, starting from an open-ended question, Gamio's ideas were condensed into a theory which in turn provided the guidelines for his research and analysis.
> ...While it is certain that the integral method developed by Manuel Gamio is a valuable anthropological contribution in the broadest sense, it is really the result of theories on which this method constantly pivots. The theoretical perspective itself is global, and thus the method is subordinated to it.[35]

b) RESEARCH

In order to complete his research on each of the defined areas—territory and population—Gamio split the area up into various sectors, and assigned each one to a specialist. While the opening "Introduction, Synthesis and Conclusions" provides a broad prospect of the research program (it was in fact Gamio's doctorate thesis

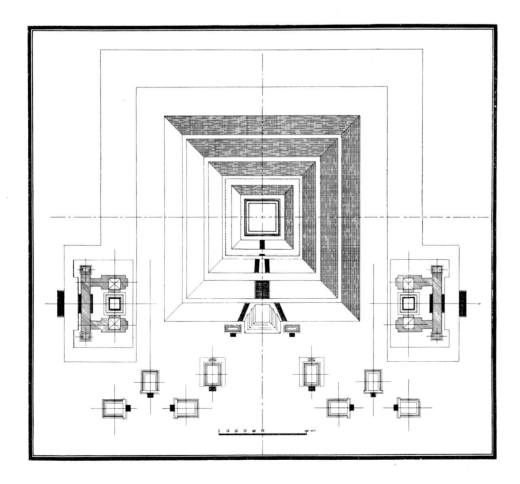

13. Reconstructed plan of the Sun Pyramid (from Gamio, 1922, Plate 37).

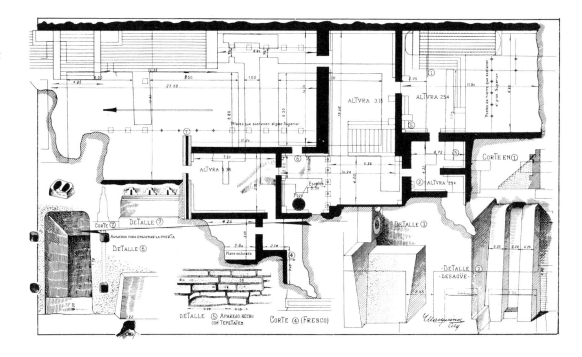

14. Plan and details of the Subterráneos (or Superimposed Buildings east of the Avenue of the Dead) drawn by Ignacio Marquina (from Gamio, 1922, Plate 17).

15. Two stone jaguars, profile and front view (from Gamio, 1922, Plate 25).

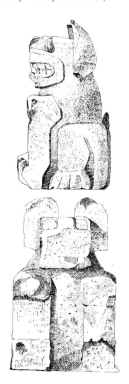

presented in 1921 at Columbia University), I will sketch the program's overall structure to clarify Gamio's working criteria and shed light on its interdisciplinary aspects. The publication opens with the introduction and conclusions mentioned above. The study proper begins in Part One, which deals first with the physical and biological aspects of the areas under study, especially their geographical and geological characteristics. These were analyzed by Ezequiel Ordóñez, at the time Director of the Instituto Geológico de México. The next topic covers the flora and fauna of the region, the former undertaken by C. Gonzatti, M. Herrera, I. Ochoterena, and J. M. Noriega, the latter, by F. Gutiérrez, M. Morfín, C. Cuesta, and M. Herrera (who had, without doubt, worked with Gamio earlier in identifying the serpent sculptures of the Templo Mayor in Tenochtitlan, discussed earlier). Flora and fauna are listed with both common and scientific names for each item classified.

The second section of the work is devoted to the Pre-Hispanic populations. First, there is a detailed account of the physical types and documented skull conformations for that period, based on three kinds of skull: those stored in the Museo Nacional (for this particular data, Gamio engaged the professional advice of Nicolás León, who concluded that the specimens were of little scientific use for this study); two skulls—one male, one female—found in burials at Teotihuacán and duly examined by Alex Hrdlicka of the National Museum of Washington; other skulls unearthed during excavation work on the Ciudadela. Next is a study by Roque Ceballos Novelo on cultural topics, including the etymology of the name Teotihuacán, and the various beliefs, myths and empirical knowledge of the Teotihuacán people.

The section on architecture which follows includes surveys of the terrain, building techniques, decoration, and overlaying of structures, as well as detailed accounts of previous studies and those carried out by the Dirección de Antropología (some of the schemes were developed by architect Ignacio Marquina). Ezequiel Ordóñez gives an analysis of indigenous sculpture (dealing with some of the raw materials used), and other specialists, such as Hermann Beyer and Gamio, provide interpretations on the type and meaning of specimens, and studies of minor sculptural works. Finally, Moisés Herrera gives a thorough breakdown of the fauna and flora.

One of the most intriguing aspects of the work is the stratigraphic analysis of Teotihuacán's cultural expansion. Gamio himself ran some of the special layer studies which included digging out sixteen shafts for a total of nine and a half square miles, exposing layers that varied between four and eight inches thick. The report, prepared by Reygadas Vértiz, shows the cross sections and measurements for each shaft dug. One of the more astonishing though mistaken conclusions was that the pottery found in Teotihuacán was contemporary with that of the Aztecs. Hermann Beyer, however, in his analysis of the similarities and difference between the two kinds of cultures, concludes that Teotihuacán culture predated Aztec culture. The Pre-Hispanic section culminates in a study by Ceballos Novelo and Beyer on the post-Teotihuacán population.

Further Excavations and Studies

After the release of Gamio's monumental study, the city of Teotihuacán received a great deal of attention from experts. A scholar from the Ethnographical Museum of Sweden, Sigvald Linné,[36] published two separate accounts, in 1939 and 1942 respectively, of his research northeast of the city and in the smaller complexes of Xolalpan and Tlamimilolpa. Other experts, such as Eduardo Noguera[37] and George Vaillant,[38] attempted to unravel the chronology of Teotihuacán.

In the 1940s new digs brought important new evidence. Excavations by Alfonso Caso[39] at Tepantitla, one of the town's districts, uncovered the famous Tlalocan Mural, which depicted aspects of daily life in the city, irrigation canals, crops of maize, beans, *nopal* (prickly pear), different species of flowers, together with butterflies and dragonflies, and games, as well as different kinds of dress. These murals provide a rich array of details on the people of Teotihuacán. Another key study, conducted by Pedro Armillas[40] along the Avenue of the Dead in the complex known as the Viking Group (named after the foundation which commissioned the excavation), made it possible to fix the dates and chronology of the settlement's physical development.

A great many further excavations in the 1950s included new work in the districts of Atetelco and Zacuala. Investigations were made into irrigation, and René Millon[41] made a thorough study of the techniques used in the Teotihuacán Valley.

Three large-scale projects carried out in the 1960s were of inestimable value in understanding Teotihuacán. These were the Proyecto Teotihuacán of the Instituto Nacional de Antropología e Historia of Mexico City, directed by Ignacio Bernal; the Teotihuacán Valley Project, by William Sanders for the Pennsylvania State University, and the Teotihuacán Mapping Project, by René Millon for Rochester University.

The Proyecto Teotihuacán

This project stemmed from studies carried out by Jorge Acosta[42] in the early 1960s on the west flank of the Plaza de la Luna (or Moon Square). Acosta unearthed three buildings situated on the square's border, and found a courtyard in the building at the southwest corner, complete with decorated pillars. Today the building is known as the Palacio del Quetzalpapalotl (or Palace of the Quetzal-Butterfly). From 1962 to 1964 additional funds made possible an even larger program of excavation for this complex and for the Avenue of the Dead. In all, eleven new sites were opened, covering the full length of the Avenue from the Plaza de la Luna to the Ciudadela.

16. Plan showing the Plaza de la Luna and the Palacio del Quetzalpapalotl or "Quetzal-Butterfly," Proyecto Teotihuacán excavations 1962-64 (from Acosta, 1964).

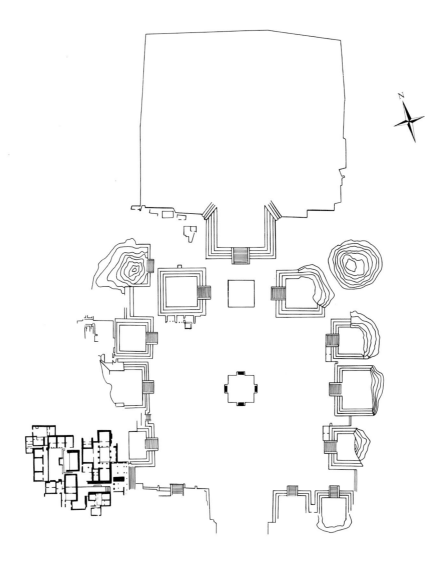

Other contributions to the program included the work of Laurette Sejourné[43] in Tetitla, a district of Teotihuacán, and work was concluded at La Ventilla, another complex southwest of the city. Among the many significant results was a better knowledge of the imposing Plaza de la Luna and the Palacio del Quetzalpapalotl, which was superimposed on another complex now known as the Palacio de los Caracoles Emplumados (or Plumed Snail Palace), obviously built earlier. The two buildings represent sophisticated examples of the kind of home reserved for the nobility or the high-ranking priesthood. At the southwest corner of the Plaza de la Luna a large ramp of steps leads into the Palacio del Quetzalpapalotl, first to a vestibule and then to the main courtyard. The courtyard has a roofed porch on all four sides, supported by pilasters carved with bird motifs, which look directly onto three apartments. The Palacio de los Caracoles Emplumados is situated directly below, and boasts a pillared facade adorned with snails bearing traces of their original coloring. The base of this complex is enhanced with polychrome murals, showing a hovering green bird with a jet of water issuing from its beak onto a flower.

Besides exposing some typical specimens of architecture, the excavations on the Avenue of the Dead have provided a great deal more data, including several highly elaborate murals. The same can be said of the excavations in Tetitla and La Ventilla. The latter site yielded several burials under the finely plastered floors.

Unfortunately, not all the finds of the Proyecto have been published.[44] It is a shame there is still no general appraisal of the area, and no use has been made of the new techniques capable of shedding more light on the city's past.

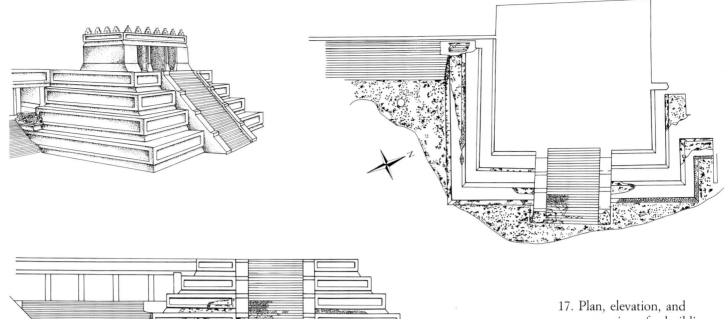

17. Plan, elevation, and reconstruction of a building in the Plaza de la Luna, with nearby steps up to the Palacio del Quetzalpapalotl, Proyecto Teotihuacán excavations 1962-64 (from Acosta, 1964).

The Teotihuacán Valley Project

In 1965 William Sanders and his team published the preliminary findings of their work on the Teotihuacán Valley,[45] supported by Pennsylvania State University. The project is basically a survey of the land's surface and includes a number of excavations to determine the distribution of the various settlements. The point of departure for Sanders' project was the symbiosis between separate regions, a theory that has been confirmed by later studies, such as those of Parsons and others in equally important regions, as in Texcoco for instance.

One of the most stimulating finds by Sanders and his team was the discovery of a village near Teotihuacán, complete with a set of living complexes. The village, named TC8, is three miles west of the Sun Pyramid. Wrote Saunders:

> One surprising result of the digs, in contrast with the common view of Mesoamerican society in the Classical period, is the clear evidence of the village's military importance. Obsidian blades were found everywhere, and were most likely spear tips.[46]

According to Sanders, Teotihuacán society in the Classical period was not a technocracy under the control of the religious elite. It is more likely that war was of paramount importance. We will be exploring this probability in depth further on.

The Teotihuacán Mapping Project and Other Recent Research

Under the guidance of René Millon,[47] this project was aimed principally at developing a map of Teotihuacán on a 1:2000 scale. To achieve this goal, a combination of methods was used, including aerial photography, the survey of a large area split up into plots approximately 1,625 feet square, and sample section excavations at various points for clues to the various stages of development of Teotihuacán and to its population and chronology. Results of the study revealed a great deal more about the city's evolution. In the next chapter we will discuss Millon's findings in more detail.

There have been other breakthroughs on Teotihuacán in the last two decades. In the early 1970s Jorge Acosta found a cavity under the Sun Pyramid. This grotto, a narrow corridor over 325 feet long, ends in a large clover-leaf design, with a series of hollows reminiscent of the mythical town Chicomoztoc. Some stretches of the wall are finished in plaster, and there are signs of an underground waterway. Various authors have stressed the unusual significance of this grotto, given that the Sun Pyramid itself was built over it.

More recently, scholars have been concentrating their research on the different aspects of the city: its pottery (Evelyn Rattray),[48] the environment (Emily McClung)[49] and the myriad fragments of obsidian (Michael Spence).[50] A computerized breakdown of the distribution of specific materials has been completed (including Cowgill's analysis of pottery remains);[51] and of course there is the Proyecto Arqueológico Teotihuacán[52] set up by the Instituto Nacional de Antropología e Historia in 1980, which focuses on the Ciudadela and a stretch of the Avenue of the Dead (see Appendix). These projects, which are still under way, should provide a wealth of new information on the city.

Chapter Three
THE CITY

Location and Environmental Features

The Teotihuacán Valley, which lies northeast of Lake Texcoco, is from 7,300 to 9,300 feet above sea level. It nestles between three major hills, Cerro Gordo (north), Cerro Patlachique (south), and Cerro Chiconautla (west), and its eastern border is demarcated by a chain of *lomas* or long hills lower than the neighboring *cerros*. Its volcanoes include Cerro Malinalco (northwest of Teotihuacán), which seems to be geologically the oldest.

The inhabitants of Teotihuacán made a wide range of important working materials from the volcanic rock in the hillsides. Obsidian from Cerro Soltepec was later used to manufacture such implements as razors and spearheads. Porous volcanic rock, *tezontle*, a primary material for building and for tools, was particularly abundant north of Santiago Tolma. This area also provided the mineral pigments used for dyestuffs.

The main source of water to the area is supplied by three rivers, the San Juan, the Huixulco, and the San Lorenzo, which passed through the village of San Juan Teotihuacán before flowing into Lake Texcoco. The various springs in San Juan and Puxtla were used to irrigate the fields and are still a chief source of water to this day.

These sources were extensively exploited by the inhabitants of Teotihuacán. They constructed an elaborate canal system to take advantage of the San Juan river. Over the years, the system underwent various changes, since the river passed right through the city from east to west, cutting between the Ciudadela complex and the 1917 Group complex, and crossing the Avenue of the Dead before joining the Huixulco and San Lorenzo rivers.

As for the springs, their position southwest of today's excavated zone may have been a determining feature in Pre-Hispanic times. An indication of their importance can be found in the Tlalocan Mural in Tepantitla, mentioned earlier: its bottom right-hand corner shows a copious stream issuing from a spring and flowing down toward what has been identified as a system of *chinampas*[1] (parcels of land surrounded by canals)—a common sight in the area even to this day. The hills probably had a rich mantle of pines, oaks, and other tree species, including conifers, identified from remains as *Taxodium mucronatum Ten* (savin, known as *ahuehuete*

18. Lake Texcoco and Teotihuacán Valley. The lake comprised stagnant saltwater and freshwater from springs.

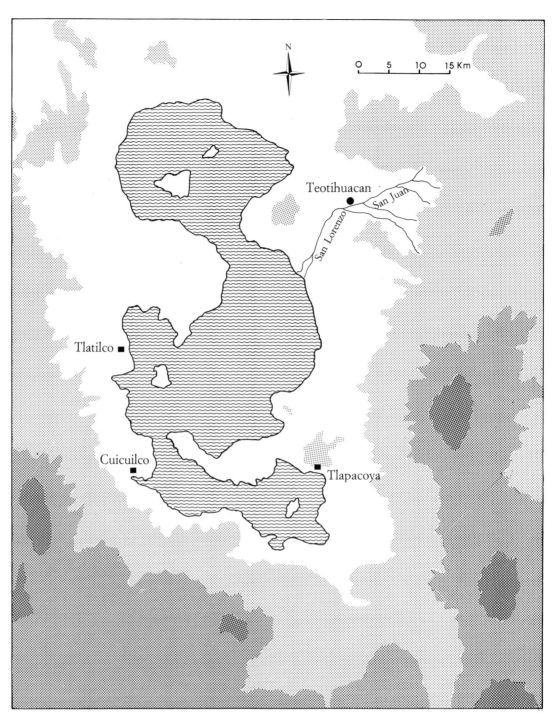

19. Three flower motifs. Molded terracotta details for application. Teotihuacán (from Gamio, 1922, Fig. 44).

20. Reconstruction from a terracotta fragment, probably the lid of a jar, with engraved scorpion decoration (from Gamio, 1922, Fig. 43).

in Náhuatl), and a variety of cyprus (or cedar), which has also turned up in excavations. *Ahuehuetes* and willow trees grew on the riverbanks, while the flat areas were used for grazing and pasture.

The Teotihuacán made extensive use of the wood from these trees, especially for building—so much so that the woodlands were soon depleted, causing an environmental change which was one of the prime causes of the city's collapse.

Clues on the fauna existing at the time are found in the murals and in pottery decoration. Remains of bones have also turned up during excavations. It is thought that a fair range of birds inhabited the valley—among them, barn owls, eagles, sparrow-hawks, wild turkeys (known as *guajolote*), and doves. The paintings also document species now atypical to the area, such as the quetzal, which today inhabits Chiapas and Guatemala. Animals in the area included deer, hares, coyotes and especially jaguars.

21. Fragment of mural with plant and flower motifs. Height 13½ inches. Museo Nacional de Antropología, Mexico City.

Various animal remains dating from the time of Teotihuacán have been found in the grotto at La Nopalera (Hidalgo), including the bones of rabbits, deer, hares, squirrels, moles, wild boars and *neotoma* (a kind of rat). Most of the remains found belong to the first two species.

Teotihuacán artwork also includes reptiles, rattlesnakes in particular. With Lake Texcoco so near, fishing and collecting water-snails were widespread activities, as shown in a mural at Tetitla, which depicts a man in the water gathering snails in a net. Other murals show insects, such as butterflies and dragonflies. All these elements give a strikingly expressive idea of the ecology of the area in which Teotihuacán culture developed, and of how the inhabitants exploited the resources around them.

The Birth of the City

In my opinion, one of the vital features of the environment affecting the development of the city of Teotihuacán is the concentration of fresh water springs in the southwest. This phenomenon has generated a series of what I call "green areas." Today these areas are strikingly different from the other, drier and hence uncultivated areas, owing to their constant supply of fresh water, which results in an abundant and constant plant growth.

Water was obviously an absolute necessity for farming peoples such as the Teotihuacán. But despite the ready supply of water, the land was by no means easy to farm, as it was originally marshland. To reclaim this land for agricultural use and channel the spring water required the constant and concerted effort of the entire community. It is very probable that the exploitation of this marshland for farming became increasingly vital, and that the site of the first settlement was decided by the environmental conditions—i.e., the people chose a spot where the land was stable and the water supply could be used to greatest advantage.

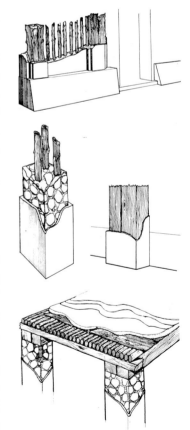

22. In Teotihuacán timber was used for building walls, pillars and roofing (from Acosta, 1964, Fig. 101).

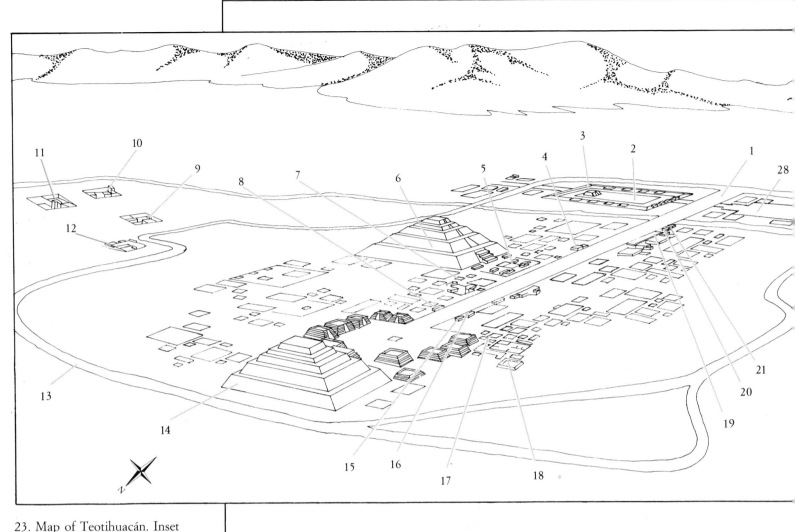

23. Map of Teotihuacán. Inset shows ceremonial precinct and residential sections. 1) Avenue of the Dead. 2) Ciudadela. 3) Templo de Quetzalcoatl. 4) Viking Group. 5) Palacio in front of the Sun Pyramid. 6) Sun Pyramid. 7) Palacio del Sol. 8) Jaguar Mural. 9) Xolalpan. 10) Merchants' Quarter. 11) Tlamimilolpa. 12) Tepantitla. 13) Modern roadway. 14) Moon Pyramid. 15) Templo de la Agricultura. 16) Templo de los Animales Mitológicos. 17) Palacio del Quetzalpapalotl (Quetzal-Butterfly) and underlying Palacio de los Caracoles Emplumados. 18) Patio de los Jaguares. 19) West Plaza Complex of the Avenue of the Dead. 20) Superimposed Buildings. 21) Northwest Complex of the San Juan river. 22) Yayahuala. 23) Zacuala. 24) Atetelco. 25) Tetitla. 26) San Juan river. 27) East-West Avenue. 28) Market.

Cerro Gordo

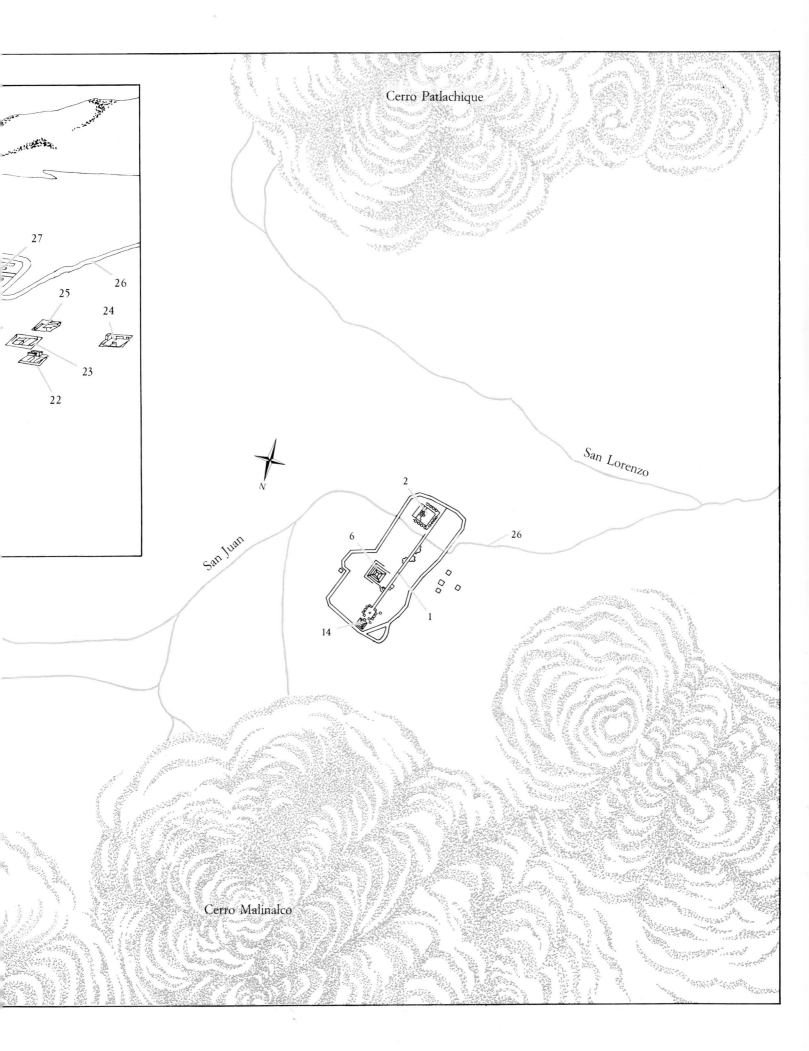

Cerro Patlachique

San Lorenzo

27

26

25

24

23

22

N

San Juan

2

6

26

1

14

Cerro Malinalco

47

There was also a mythical element in this choice of a site. Apparently the underground water grotto was an important feature of the Sun Pyramid. Every decision of the settlers was clearly made in the context of a complex set of vital economic and mythological factors, and the city was founded on this site around the time of the birth of Christ.

In the centuries immediately preceding the city's foundation, the Teotihuacán Valley inhabitants developed a complex technology which enabled them to turn the environment to good advantage. In Cuicuilco, for example, there is a large base nearly 500 feet across, resembling the small volcanoes found in the vicinity. As for "green areas," it is probable that, before the volcano Xitle destroyed Cuicuilco in 200 B.C., there were extensive farm lands irrigated with water from the rivers crisscrossing the region, and perhaps even plentiful springs like those in nearby Tlalpan today.

A similar pattern has been detected in the Puebla Valley, where a town called Cholula grew and thrived contemporary with Teotihuacán. Here there are several springs generating a "green area" northeast of the town's main pyramid. The area was undoubtedly important in the first phase of the town's development.

Excavations in Teotihuacán have revealed another significant clue on the function of water sources. In the murals at Tepantitla, which date back to approximately A.D. 500, there is a scene supposedly depicting the nether world of the rain god (known as Tlalocan, after the rain god Tlaloc), though some experts consider it a scene from everyday life presided over by the rain god. On the opposite wall, the scene continues with a set of small pockets of land painted green, with crops including maize, squash, *nopal*, and agave. These curious plots are marked off with symmetrical bands of blue, as if representing the typical irrigation canals of the *chinampas*.

In the bottom right corner of the famous Tlalocan scene we can see what Alfonso Caso[2] has interpreted as an island with a frog perched in its center. We have reinterpreted it as a spring, because it is from this spot that the water flows out to form the system of *chinampas* depicted on the opposite wall.

Southwest of the ceremonial center of Teotihuacán there is an area resembling those depicted in the mural, which would seem to indicate the use of *chinampas* in Pre-Hispanic times, as in later periods.

5. The inner courtyard of the Palacio del Quetzalpapalotl, or "Quetzal-Butterfly." Xolalpan Phase, A.D. 450-650. Detail of painted cornice and two "almenas" or merlons crowning the building's roof, engraved with bas-relief designs symbolizing the year.

Following pages:

6. The Avenue of the Dead. Built in successive periods and completed in the Xolalpan Phase, A.D. 450-650, the Avenue cuts north-south through the city. The Avenue runs 1¹/₄ miles from the Moon Pyramid to the Ciudadela, and then continues south for another 1¹/₄ miles. On the right, the Moon Pyramid.

7. Polychrome mural on the east side of the Avenue of the Dead featuring a huge jaguar. Length 6 feet. Xolalpan Phase, A.D. 450-650. The diagonal bands and circles symbolize rain.

8. Temples along the Avenue of the Dead.

9. Building along the Avenue of the Dead.

Opposite:

10. *Palace in front of the Sun Pyramid, adjacent to the Avenue of the Dead.*

11. *Rooms of the Palace in front of the Sun Pyramid.*

12. *The Palacio del Sol, a residential building on the northwest side of the Sun Pyramid.*

13. *Inner courtyard of the Palacio del Sol.*

Following pages:

14. *The Sun Pyramid, north face. Base ca. 738 feet square, height 213 feet (originally comprised a temple crowning the summit, 249 feet high). The pyramid dates from the Tzacualli Phase, A.D. 1-150, and is seen here from the Plaza de la Luna.*

15. *A close-up of the Sun Pyramid walls, made of large blocks of volcanic rock, viewed from below.*

16. *The Moon Pyramid, south face, and the Plaza de la Luna, seen from the summit of the Sun Pyramid.*

17. *The Ciudadela, north view from the summit of the Sun Pyramid. Miccaotli-Tlamimilolpa Phases, A.D. 150-450.*

18. The altar at the center of the Ciudadela. Behind this, the building with four "talud-tablero" levels built over the Templo de Quetzalcoatl, the tip of which is just visible.

Opposite:

19. Detail of the altar at the center of the Ciudadela. In the background, the north side of the raised Gran Plataforma enclosing the Ciudadela.

Following pages:

20. The altar at the center of the Ciudadela clearing, seen from the west.

21. The raised Gran Plataforma enclosing the Ciudadela, seen from inside. Note the three double orders of steps and three pyramid bases.

22. Polychrome mural on a building within the Ciudadela.

René Millon, who has carried out extensive studies into the layout of Teotihuacán and its environs, seems to confirm this idea:

> It is likely that a system of *chinampas* answered most of the food needs of the city of Teotihuacán. The Teotihuacán Valley is somewhat limited in size to fulfill the city's needs at the height of its splendor. Even if it had sufficed, it is an unproven factor we have not yet managed to clarify.[3]

Among the scholars involved in studying the Teotihuacán farming systems, archaeologist William Sanders[4] claims that the wet region southwest of Teotihuacán suggests a system of *chinampas* in use when the city was at its zenith. Manuel Gamio[5] also refers to this area, noting that many irrigation canals have been found there.

Opposite:

23. Right, the Templo de Quetzalcoatl. 208 feet square. Miccaotli Phase, A.D. 150-250. Left, building with four "talud-tablero" levels which in the successive Tlamimilolpa Phase covered the temple completely.

25. Map of Teotihuacán drawn by René Millon (from Millon, 1973).

Evidence suggests that the site had characteristics which singled it out as ideal for the cradle of a vast culture. But the internal organization of the society itself was very decisive too. Work both in the countryside and in the city was carefully structured, with such methods as the calculated distribution of land, and the plan of urban expansion into four large neighborhoods spreading outward from the central focus of a religious precinct marked by imposing causeways.

The mixture of natural physical needs and a complex set of myths (which we are able to understand today owing to our knowledge of the economy and the remains of Teotihuacán's thriving culture) combined to create the first full-fledged city in the Central Plateau.

During the phases in which some of the settlements scattered around Lake Texcoco became major centers of culture, others seem to be of no importance whatsoever. After Cuicuilco was destroyed by volcanic eruption, Teotihuacán began to grow in power and importance. Let us now look at the entire cycle of development of this city, from its foundation to its apogee as the City of Gods.

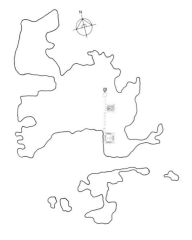

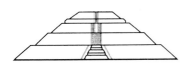

26. Urban expansion during the Tzacualli Phase.

PATLACHIQUE PHASE
(100-0 B.C.)

According to the studies of René Millon[6] and his group, during this phase there were two sizable settlements covering over two and a half square miles each, and two smaller ones. The first two were sited north of the future city. One of them covered part of the ceremonial area, where the Avenue of the Dead was later built. It would not be surprising if some of the temples found later actually date from this period and were among the older buildings in the city's sacred area.

The population during this period has been calculated at around five thousand.

TZACUALLI PHASE
(A.D. 1-150)

In this phase, the main characteristics of the emerging culture of Teotihuacán were established.

The route of what would later become the Avenue of the Dead was prepared, together with the East-West Avenue.

The vast Moon and Sun pyramids date from this period, and there is a strong possibility that the exact position of the Sun Pyramid was decided by a natural underground grotto over 330 feet long, where geologists suggest there was a subterranean river at some stage. The discovery of a water supply—an essential asset for a predominantly farming population—was evidently highly symbolic, and may well have spurred the town's inhabitants to site the pyramid over this mysterious water source. Whatever inspired their decision, we know that in Pre-Hispanic culture grottoes were considered strongly symbolic of birth and death.

Also belonging to this phase is a complex in typical Teotihuacán style, comprised of three temples, though some examples of these religious structures are known to belong to the previous phase.

During the Tzacualli phase the town grew to an impressive ten to eleven square miles, with a population estimated at around thirty thousand, making it clearly one of the largest—if not the largest—inhabited centers in the Valley of Mexico. Meanwhile, in the Puebla Valley the foundations of another city of great historical importance were being laid, Cholula.

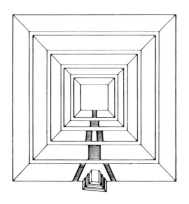

27. Elevation and plan of the Sun Pyramid.

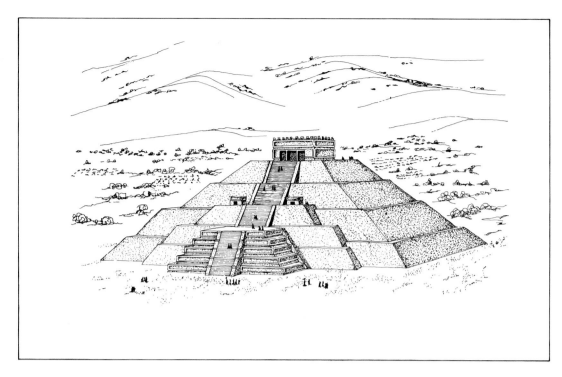

28. Reconstruction of the Moon Pyramid (from Acosta, 1978).

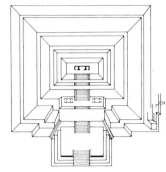

29. Elevation and plan of the Moon Pyramid.

MICCAOTLI PHASE
(A.D. 150-250)

During this phase, Teotihuacán was divided into four grand "quadrants" or neighborhoods by the great East-West Avenue and the Avenue of the Dead, which were carefully consolidated. The hub was the Ciudadela and the huge Marketplace (or Great Compound) facing it.

This phase also saw the construction of the Templo de Quetzalcoatl in the center of the vast clearing of the Ciudadela. In his commentary, Millon notes:

> It seems that this area [the Ciudadela] was the heart of the city, geographically, culturally, politically and probably even economically.[7]

It also had great religious importance. The layout of the buildings around the clearing of the Ciudadela follows a logic that has not yet been decoded, but some idea can be obtained from the characteristics of the buildings, such as the four pyramid bases or *adoratorios* arranged on each side of the huge platform enclosing

30. Urban expansion during the Miccaotli Phase.

31. Reconstruction of the Templo de Quetzalcoatl in the Ciudadela, drawn by Ignacio Marquina (from Marquina, 1951).

32. Plan of the Ciudadela.

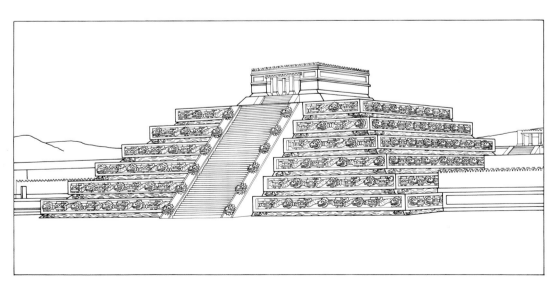

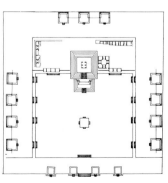

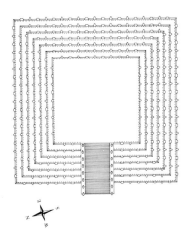

33. Plan of the Templo de Quetzalcoatl.

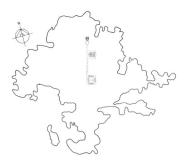

34. Urban expansion during the Tlamimilolpa Phase.

the Ciudadela, except on the east side, where there are only three bases—a somewhat puzzling arrangement which deserves looking into in greater depth.

At the height of its glory, the city is thought to have covered an area of over fourteen square miles, and its population stood at approximately forty-five thousand (and had by no means reached its peak). It would appear that Teotihuacán at its peak was even greater than imperial Rome, though Millon considers this unlikely, and sets its population at less than one-fifth that of Rome.

TLAMIMILOLPA PHASE
(A.D. 250-450)

During this phase, the city began to grow in on itself, in the sense that many new buildings were constructed over preceding ones. This is noticeable in the Ciudadela, where the magnificent Templo de Quetzalcoatl, with its polychrome decorations of huge serpents, snails and shells, was covered by a series of constructions built with the *talud-tablero* technique (alternating aprons and panel blocks). Another important artifact of the period is the mural, depicting birds in flight, in the basement of the Palacio de los Caracoles Emplumados (Plumed Snail Palace), situated below the Palacio del Quetzalpapalotl, at the southwestern corner of the Plaza de la Luna. Several other murals and their support walls date from this phase, such as those in the Templo de la Agricultura, and, close by, the murals in the Templo de los Animales Mitológicos, all found along the Avenue of the Dead. This last set of paintings is particularly interesting, providing, as its name suggests, a painted scenario of several key Teotihuacán myths.

Some of the residential complexes date from this phase too, including the Tlamimilolpa site excavated by Sigvald Linné. Apparently the city developed in blocks or neighborhoods connected by narrow alleys. There are also signs of links with the Maya and other coastal cultures native to the Gulf of Mexico.

While the population increased to sixty-five thousand, the city itself actually shrank in size to under fourteen square miles.

35. Palacio de los Caracoles Emplumados, with details of the murals of birds in flight (see Plates 58, 59).

XOLALPAN PHASE
(A.D. 450-650)

During this phase, the entire Valley of Mexico and surrounding areas reached a peak of splendor and prosperity. In the city, the Avenue of the Dead and the neighboring ritual and residential precincts assumed the configuration they have today. Residential complexes initiated in the previous phase underwent extension, including Tetitla, Yayahuala, Atetelco, Tepantitla, Xolalpan, Tlamimilolpa, and the Palacio del Quetzalpapalotl; many of them were encircled by walls creating neighborhood blocks approximately two hundred feet square. At this juncture the city must have an impressive sight, with its imposing ritual area along the Avenue of the Dead and many residential complexes, each with one or two access points.

The elaborately designed interiors had rooms and areas centered on small open courtyards providing light and enabling rainwater to be collected and channeled through a system of underground ducts. Rooms were linked by narrow corridors, and occasionally connected to small inner temples or similar places of worship, as at Tetitla. Walls were embellished with painted designs, and on rare occasions even the floors show traces of decoration. The blocks themselves were crisscrossed with interconnecting roads. Some of the streets may have comprised a combination of road and waterway, as suggested by a mural in Tetitla, which shows a kneeling figure dressed as a jaguar, heading toward a temple (his route is suggested by footprints),

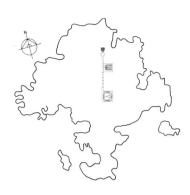

36. Urban expansion during the Xolalpan Phase.

37. Plan of Tetitla, a residential section of Teotihuacán.

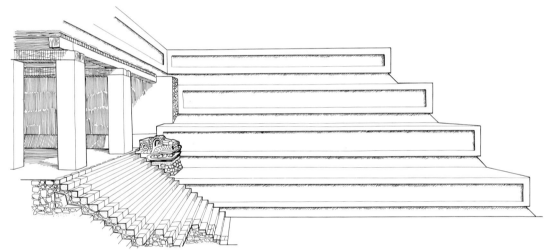

38. Entrance to the Palacio del Quetzalpapalotl with large serpent head at one side of stairway (see Plate 48) (from Acosta, 1964).

39. Patio de los Jaguares behind the Palacio del Quetzalpapalotl. In the background, the Moon Pyramid.

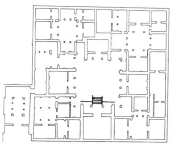

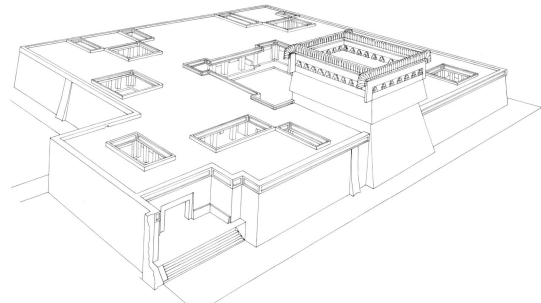

40. 41. Plan and reconstruction of Zacuala, a residential section of Teotihuacán.

along a causeway flanked on either side by a canal. The city, with its religious center, administrative buildings, and living quarters, was a complex feat of engineering, as was the vast network of canals and underground ducts connected with the river cutting through the city. Large reservoirs of water for common use have been discovered in the residential blocs. Also belonging to this era was the construction of the Great Compound facing the Ciudadela, which Millon reckons was the site of the marketplace. He has pointed out the marked differences in architecture between the Great Compound and the Ciudadela. While the latter was reserved for religious purposes, the former may well have had a civil function. Both these central precincts were of vital importance to Teotihuacán.

Murals were clearly a significant feature of the architecture, and were displayed throughout Teotihuacán. Some of the more important ones were painted during this phase, such as the the great jaguar mural in the Avenue of the Dead; the puma murals in Tetitla; the murals in the Palacio de Zacuala; the Tlalocan Mural at Tepantitla, and also the Tepantitla mural depicting priests scattering seeds on the ground. Dating from a little later in the same phase are the murals in the courtyard known as the Patio Blanco in Atetelco and the Patio de los Jaguares behind the Palacio del Quetzalpapalotl. Also dating from toward the close of this phase are the murals in the Palacio del Quetzalpapalotl, as well as those in the upper layer of Tetitla and in the Patio Pintado in Atetelco.

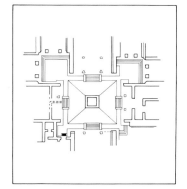

42. 43. Plan of the Patio Central and reconstruction of the Patio Blanco (from Coe, 1964), both at Atetelco, a residential section of Teotihuacán.

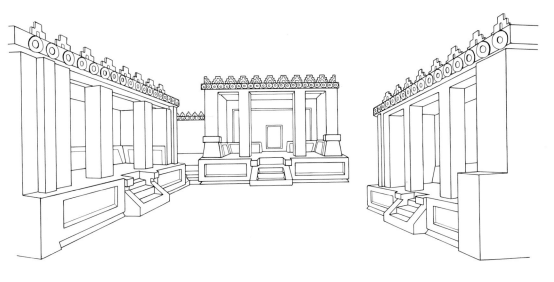

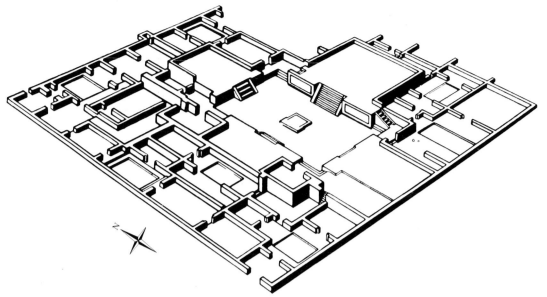

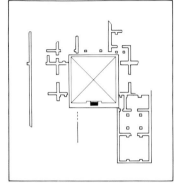

44. Perspective plan of Xolalpan, a residential section of Teotihuacán (from Willey, 1966).

45. Plan of a building at Tepantitla, a residential section of Teotihuacán.

By this time, the city's population had reached its peak, with some eighty-five thousand inhabitants, though the city's size was less than thirteen square miles.

METEPEC PHASE
(A.D. 650-750)

There are telltale signs of decline in the hundred years before the city was destroyed. Evidence suggests that it had shrunk, particularly on the south side, and now covered a mere twelve and a half square miles. The population had also dwindled to about seventy thousand (the waning strength of the city was to have significant repercussions on the whole of Mesoamerica in the eighth century A.D.). The population suddenly plummeted in the succeeding Oxtotipac Phase, leaving Teotihuacán with a mere two to five thousand inhabitants.

But what exactly were the causes that triggered the decline and eventual demise of Teotihuacán toward A.D. 750?

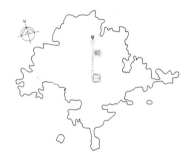

46. Urban expansion during the Metepec Phase.

A City Destroyed

Many excavations and studies on the ceremonial area have revealed numerous signs of fire damage, collapsed roofs, holes in floors and courtyards. The impression is one of a sudden and even violent end to the city.

Concerted efforts have been made to try to unravel this final phase of the city. Some of the theories advanced—such as the idea of an earthquake or plague—are untenable owing to the lack of sufficient data. One theory is that races from the north invaded the city and razed it. Others have suggested that the farming population rose up against the elite priesthood. I find none of these explanations plausible, and the question needs careful examination.

To my mind, the decline of Teotihuacán's glory is directly linked to the emergence of stratified societies in Mesoamerica, which came about around the year 1000 B.C. The Olmec were a typical example of this new breed of society. They were governed by a powerful minority who controlled every aspect of civil and religious life. The existence of stratified societies is demonstrated by the presence of buildings and sculptural works denoting the religious powers wielded by a small social group.

47. Figure dressed as a jaguar, surrounded by glyphs. Detail from the murals at Cacaxtla, a site in the state of Tlaxcala.

Supporting evidence has turned up in Central Mexico, particularly in Tlapacoya and Cuicuilco. In Teotihuacán, signs of the growing hierarchy increased in a later era. I believe that farming was a key factor in Teotihuacán's economy and that the control of water grew in political and economic importance. Unlike most other scholars, I believe that the other crucial economic factor was war, and that during this period the farming economy was gradually integrated with the acquisition and control of new lands and tributary areas, a development that is intrinsic to all the later history of Mesoamerica, as clearly evidenced in the Postclassic era. Curiously, studies of Classic societies like that of Teotihuacán have paid scant attention to military questions and war, in spite of the archaeological finds in the Puebla and Tlaxcala regions. Complexes with walls or protective trenches were common in these regions, probably serving as a means of defense against Teotihuacán expansionism. Murals found in Cacaxtla depict the last hundred years of Teotihuacán as beset by ethnic struggles. Excavations of Maya areas of the same date have revealed murals featuring figures armed with spears, dragging their slain enemies by the hair. So much for the idea of pacific races ruled by the priesthood!

All this has led me to believe that the characteristic to look for in these early stratified societies—as in the case of Teotihuacán in its relations with its neighbors— was the aggressive pursuit of new races to conquer for tax reasons, a phenomenon that would become dominant in later Mesoamerica. Such aggressive moves led to deep resentment among vassal tribes, coupled with the nagging desire to rid themselves of their overlords. The entire history of Central Mexico testifies to this.

The Aztecs themselves began as a subject race in the thirteenth century A.D.: they were forced to pay taxes and their able-bodied men had to fight as mercenaries in expansionist campaigns for their rulers. Eventually the Aztecs rebelled, joined forces with other vassal races and routed their oppressors. The roles were thus reversed, and the Aztec population rose to power, exacting tributes from those who had once ruled over them. Inevitably, the new subject races expanded, and the balance of power once more became precarious. The Aztecs subjugated a great many racial groups, and when the Spanish conquistadores penetrated the mainland, the oppressed were easily enlisted to rise up against their oppressors. And so history repeated itself, and the native races joined forces with the Spanish invaders and mercilessly struck down their Aztec overlords.

This historical cycle, typical of Central Mexico since the eleventh century (as proved by the available historical sources and archaeological finds), may have its origins in much earlier times. In Teotihuacán's case, for instance, the rapid expansion of the prospering city was also due to the constant military expansionist effort. As a result, in the eighth century, vassals rose against their masters, burned Teotihuacán to the ground and thus freed themselves from the terrible yoke imposed on them by their oppressors, who were already caught in an inexorable decline. The later history of the area confirms as much. So why not acknowledge the evidence? It is all there, in the signs of fire and looting in the city, in what Millon has identified as city walls to the north, and in the fortified centers outside Teotihuacán. Why this insistence on a *pax teotihuacana* for which there is no evidence? Why ignore the historical facts?

Of all the theories regarding the fate of the city and its culture, my theory is the only one backed up by archaeological data and similar events in the area's history. Time alone will prove which theory is correct.

Whatever the truth of the matter, Teotihuacán was undoubtedly trapped in irreversible decay. The collapse of its culture signaled the end of stability in Central Mexico and the gradual resurgence of many smaller cultural units, each one vying for control over the others. These included Tula, Xochicalco, and Cacaxtla, which reached the apogee of their development between the eighth and eleventh centuries A.D., until the Aztecs began to prosper and expand in the Valley of Mexico, creating an altogether new power that was to make itself felt throughout most of Mesoamerica.

Chapter Four
STATE,
SOCIAL ORGANIZATION,
AND ECONOMY

We have seen that the city of Teotihuacán developed over a span of seven centuries. We now need to understand how it was organized socially. As explained in the last chapter, Teotihuacán was favorably sited, and its inhabitants had reached a relatively advanced stage of technology. It is important to understand both the practice of waging war and the methods of farming in the valley. From there, we can grasp the basic aims of this civilization.

The location's many "green areas" must clearly have contributed greatly to the city's development. Likewise it is clear that the various environmental features were favorable for human settlement, i.e., the site's proximity to Lake Texcoco and quarries providing building material and stone for making tools. There was also a plentiful supply of minerals, useful for the manufacture of tools and utensils. There were rivers flowing through the site and forests close by, which provided wood and wild game of all kinds. Finally, there was a plentiful supply of springs providing fresh water. Consequently, the people of Teotihuacán were in a position to use their environment to great advantage. We will now look into the city's social organization and the varied methods of production to understand the mechanisms guiding this complex society.

The State of Teotihuacán

Teotihuacán society was governed by an elite group who wielded power over its entire social structure. This is the only explanation for its advanced levels of organization. The lords of Teotihuacán had a keen knowledge of the stars, which were decisive in determining the city's physical alignment. Its wise men also developed standards for designing buildings. The marked difference between the city and the surrounding hamlets suggests the latter were small units devoted to intensive farming. Similarly, in the city itself there were specialists in various areas of production, as corroborated by the great quantity of material uncovered in the course of archaeological inquiry over the years. But the city's complex web of daily activities was embodied in the form of a full-fledged state, a unitary power that controlled its science and economy.

Just what were the main features of the Teotihuacán state? First, we should define what we mean by the term "state" in the context of Mesoamerica. As used here, it denotes a highly stratified society in which a small group rules over the masses. In Teotihuacán this elite group exploited the society's religion and art, with the support of its warrior class, which played a crucial role in the state's expansion. The inhabitants of each newly conquered region were obliged to pay taxes to the metropolis.

Indications of a stratified society are gleaned in part from archaeological discoveries and from what remains of its architecture, which help reconstruct an outline of its former magnificence. The cultural similarities between the civilization of Teotihuacán and that of another documented racial group, the Olmec, who existed one thousand years earlier, is borne out by similarities in their architecture and sculpture. Another feature showing that Teotihuacán was a stratified society ruled by a militarily powerful state is the presence of far-flung settlement areas (as in Puebla and Tlaxcala), which were forced to erect permanent defense barriers against the expansionist efforts of the main city.

In order to appreciate the scope and implications of the Teotihuacán state, we have to assess the links between the culture of the metropolis and the other cultures around it. Unfortunately, the archaeological data we have is insufficient to determine precisely whether this interaction was based on trade links or military conquest, or whether it represented simply the general influence of a major culture. The word "influence" is somewhat noncommittal if merely used to denote the presence of a given culture in territories occupied by races of different cultural stock from that of the metropolis. But it is interesting to see how a whole range of specific Teotihuacán features, such as architecture, pottery, and sculpture, have turned up in various regions in Mesoamerica.

THE CENTRAL VALLEYS AND THE TEOTLALPAN REGION

We shall begin our inquiry in the area closest to Teotihuacán, that is, the Valley of Mexico, the Puebla Valley and the Teotlalpan region (or region of Tula), north of the city. Generally speaking, available archaeological data indicate that these regions were an integral part of the Teotihuacán state.

Remains of Teotihuacán material are abundant, particularly pottery shards, and certain architectural features recur in several sites in the Puebla Valley, especially in Cholula. It is interesting to note that Cholula and Teotihuacán grew simultaneously and were based on approximately the same settlement model. As far as we know, both cities had a large population and in both there are traces of farming activity in the surrounding region. Furthermore, Cholula was a compulsory port of call for anyone traveling toward the Totonac region of what is now the state of Veracruz, or toward Oaxaca. The strategic economic and military importance of Cholula is undeniable.

Traces of Teotihuacán culture have turned up in Puebla and Tlaxcala, but there are also signs of a period in which these two regions were independent of the metropolis. Some finds suggest that, even then, a kind of Teotihuacán "corridor" existed. Other settlements were equipped with fortified defense structures, probably as a measure against the expansionist tendencies of the nearby metropolis. Tlaxcala later became increasingly independent of outside ethnic groups.

North of Teotihuacán, in sites such as Tepeapulco and Huapalcalco (in the Teotlalpan region, Hidalgo), typical Teotihuacán material has been found. Tepeapulco, for instance, lies roughly eighteen miles north of Teotihuacán and has buildings constructed on a *talud-tablero* design. The pottery remnants found there

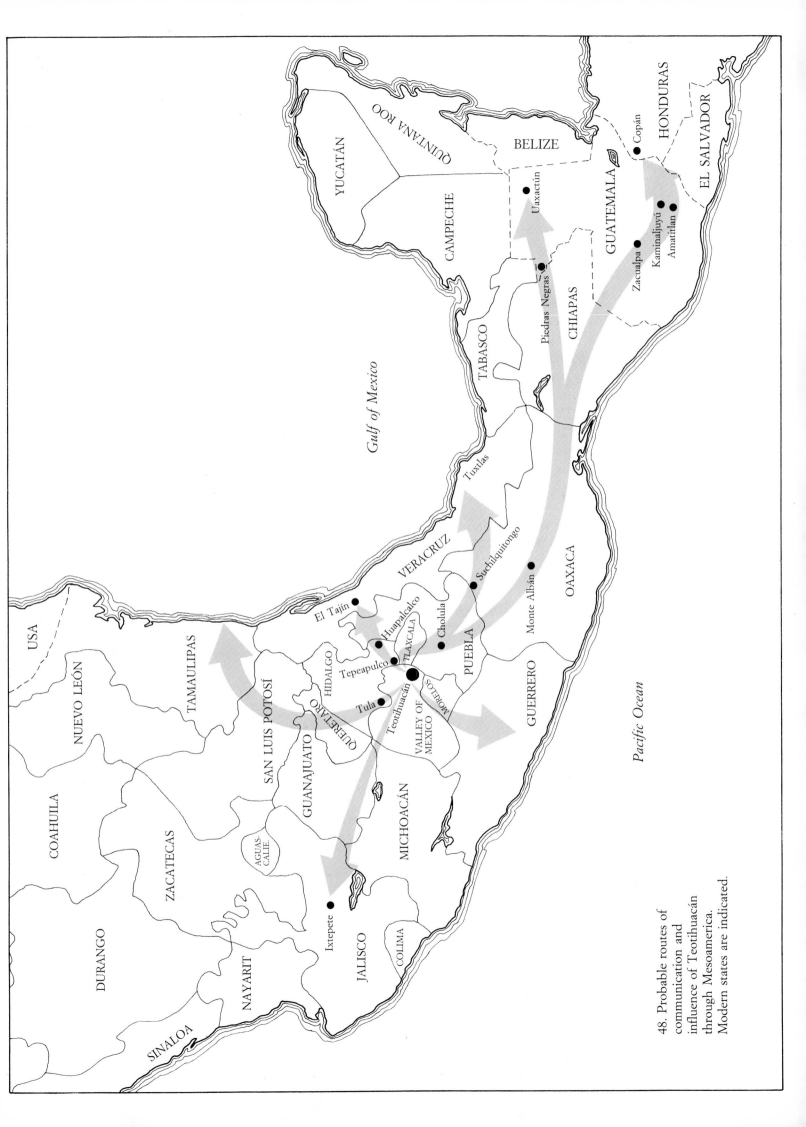

USA

COAHUILA

NUEVO LEÓN

TAMAULIPAS

DURANGO

ZACATECAS

SAN LUIS POTOSÍ

QUERÉTARO

GUANAJUATO

AGUAS. CALIE.

Ixtepete

JALISCO

COLIMA

NAYARIT

SINALOA

MICHOACÁN

Tula

HIDALGO

Tepeapulco

Teotihuacán

VALLEY OF MEXICO

MORELOS

TLAXCALA

Huapalcalco

El Tajín

VERACRUZ

Cholula

PUEBLA

GUERRERO

Suchilquitongo

Monte Albán

OAXACA

Tuxtlas

Gulf of Mexico

TABASCO

Piedras Negras

CHIAPAS

CAMPECHE

YUCATÁN

QUINTANA ROO

BELIZE

Uaxactún

GUATEMALA

Zacualpa

Kaminaljuyú

Amatitlán

Copán

HONDURAS

EL SALVADOR

Pacific Ocean

48. Probable routes of communication and influence of Teotihuacán through Mesoamerica. Modern states are indicated.

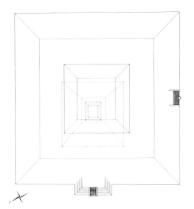

49. Reconstructed plan of the main Cholula pyramid, state of Puebla.

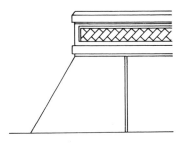

50. Local variant of the Teotihuacán *talud-tablero* system used in the Cholula pyramid.

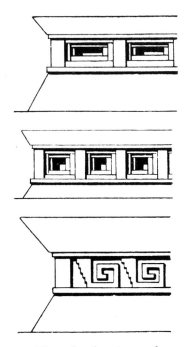

51. Three local variants of the Teotihuacán *talud-tablero* system used in the El Tajín pyramids, state of Veracruz.

are also typical of or similar to those manufactured in Teotihuacán. The causeway leading out of the small main plaza is almost a replica of the Avenue of the Dead. Wall relics and obsidian fragments have been found in the northern part. The settlement undoubtedly had a Teotihuacán population and must have been important, considering its position as an outpost to Teotihuacán toward the northeast, providing an obligatory stopover between Teotihuacán, the north of Veracruz and the Huastec culture of the Gulf Coast. Huapalcalco is equally interesting. It stood near the present-day town of Tulancingo. The distance between Teotihuacán and the two sites, Tepeapulco and Huapalcalco, is virtually the same, as if there were a set distance between the metropolis and its satellites. Excavations at Huapalcalco have yielded architecture and pottery similar to those of the metropolis, together with other objects, such as yokes, typical of the Veracruz area, which prove the existence of links with certain key centers, like El Tajín in Veracruz.

To the north of Teotihuacán lies the region of Teotlalpan (in today's state of Hidalgo), where the Toltec culture was later to develop, with its capital, Tula. But here too there is evidence of Teotihuacán settlements, just as the mother city had reached the peak of its glory. During research sponsored in the early 1970s by the Proyecto Tula, and directed by myself, a number of new sites came to light, two of which in particular (Site 83 and the Chingú site) yielded examples of pottery very similar to that of Teotihuacán.

What was the logic behind the Teotihuacán presence in this region? In 1974 we suggested that the abundance of calcareous rock in the area could have induced the Teotihuacán to take over the region. Throughout the capital there was widespread use of plaster (made from a mixture of lime, quartziferous sand and water) and it is hardly surprising that the Teotihuacán should want exclusive control over a region guaranteeing a supply of raw material in such demand in the metropolis.

THE GULF COAST (VERACRUZ)

We will now look briefly at the other far-flung (though no less important) regions in which signs of Teotihuacán culture have emerged.

We have already spoken of the probable existence of a road running from Teotihuacán through Tepeapulco and Huapalcalco toward the Totonac area in the northeast, where certain towns of considerable prominence once stood. One such town was El Tajín in Veracruz, dating from the Preclassic period, which reached the height of its development at the same time as Teotihuacán and Cholula. The area this town controlled was most likely extensive, and traces of its culture have turned up in both those cities, especially the sculpted decorative motifs and stone yokes (found in Teotihuacán). These probably originated in the central area of Veracruz, an area under the control of the city of El Tajín.

The situation in the southern area of Veracruz, however, was different. The number of Teotihuacán objects is even greater in the Tuxtlas mountains.

GUERRERO AND THE WEST

Today's state of Guerrero lies south of Teotihuacán and stretches as far as the Pacific coast. Here, fragments of sculpture and pottery have been found which indicate close ties with the metropolis, such as the stone masks, very similar in design to the magnificent samples found in Teotihuacán, and statuettes, samples of which have also been found there. We should add that this region, which was the object of repeated struggles for possession in successive epochs, is rich in greenstone

24. Tripod vase with priest scattering seeds on the ground. Terracotta with engraved decoration, height 4½ inches. Museo Nacional de Antropología, Mexico City.

25. *Fragment of tripod
vase with talking figure.
Terracotta with relief and
engraved decoration, height
7 inches. Museo Nacional de
Antropología, Mexico City.*

26. *Tripod vase with priests.*
Terracotta with relief
polychrome decoration,
height 6 inches. Museo
Nacional de Antropología,
Mexico City.

27. 28. Two priests in
procession scattering seeds on
the ground. Details from the
Tepantitla murals,
Teotihuacán.

Following pages:

29. Detail of lower panel of
the Tlalocan Mural at
Tepantitla, Teotihuacán.
Replica, Museo Nacional de
Antropología, Mexico City.
The panel is thought to
represent the paradise of the
god Tlaloc or, more probably,
scenes from earthly life
(see Figures 85 and 86
on page 178).

30. *Seated figure with
elaborate headdress.
Terracotta. Museo
Nacional de Antropología,
Mexico City.*

31. Old man. Carved and polished terracotta, height 6 inches. Museo Nacional de Antropología, Mexico City.

32. Reclining figure.
Terracotta, height 4¹/₂ inches.
Museo Nacional de
Antropología, Mexico City.

Opposite:

33. Anthropomorphic
sculpture.

34. *Effigy vessel.*
Dark terracotta, height
8 inches. Museo Nacional de
Antropología, Mexico City.

35. Effigy vessel.
Ceramic, height 7 inches
Museo Nacional de
Antropología, Mexico City.

36. *Ceramic vase.*

37. *"Candelero" or incense
burner. Terracotta,
height 2¹/₂ inches. Museo
Nacional de Antropología,
Mexico City.*

38. *"Anaranjado Delgado" or Thin Orange pottery vessel, with three tiny spherical supports called "soportes-botón."*

39. *Common bowl. Terracotta, height 8 inches. Museo Nacional de Antropología, Mexico City.*

40. *Figurine with movable limbs, perhaps used as a toy. Terracotta, height 12 inches. Museo Nacional de Antropología, Mexico City.*

deposits and important crops, such as cotton, and fruits which did not grow on the higher plateau. The area had a certain symbolic importance also, due to the sun's shift toward the south during the winter solstice. This phenomenon, which the Pre-Hispanic astronomers had already noticed, became the basis for several myths that, despite their reworking by later societies, most certainly originated with the Teotihuacán.

The region west of the metropolis also shows interesting links. Ixtepete, a site discovered near to today's Guadalajara, has yielded buildings constructed according to the Teotihuacán *talud-tablero* design, albeit with some slight variations. Other finds include ollas in the Comala style, decorated with priests dressed in typical Teotihuacán ritual gear. The technique is cruder, however.

OAXACA

Evidence of links with the central valleys of Oaxaca has also been found in Teotihuacán. It must be remembered that at the height of Teotihuacán's glory, the region of Oaxaca boasted several full-fledged towns, including Monte Albán. Certain shapes that recur in Teotihuacán pottery are evident in the Zapotec phase of Monte Albán pottery (known as Phase IIIa and Phase IIIb).

Excavations in Teotihuacán yielded the *barrio oaxaqueño* (a residential neighborhood of people from Oaxaca), where a great many objects of Oaxacan origin were unearthed. Moreover, Teotihuacán was not the only city with links to Oaxaca: in Cholula there are architectural features similar to those found in Monte Albán, though with a style of their own.

One of the roads toward the southeast of Mesoamerica winds through the Puebla Valley (touching Cholula) and thence through the central valleys of Oaxaca. Close by the mountain chain dividing Puebla from Oaxaca toward the northeast stands the site of Suchilquitongo which, given its position, may well have been a strategic township.

THE MAYA REGION

South of Chiapas and in Guatemala, certain finds have provided definitive proof of contact with Teotihuacán. More than any other site, Kaminaljuyú in the highlands of Guatemala has yielded relics in the Teotihuacán style, some imported and some local imitations. Elsewhere, as in the sites of Zacualpa and Amatitlan, similarities have also been found, though much less striking than those of Kaminaljuyú. Other sites, such as Uaxactún and Piedras Negras in the region of Petén (Guatemala) and Copán on the border between Guatemala and Honduras, testify to the influence of Teotihuacán. The relics found, particularly the pottery (though at times only in minor details) prove the existence of links with the Valley of Mexico.

The more typical features of Teotihuacán culture are therefore found in other regions of Mesoamerica, in the same way as features of other cultures have turned up in the metropolis itself. But, as explained at the start, the areas under the direct control of Teotihuacán were a section of the Valley of Mexico and the Valleys of Puebla and Tlaxcala (in both these valleys there is evidence of resistance to Teotihuacán and it has been suggested that there was a Teotihuacán "corridor" cutting through them), and the region of Teotlalpan, north of the city. There may well have been trade links with other regions, as in the case of El Tajín, Monte Albán and some Maya towns, since these towns were at the height of their development and were also obliged to control the regions around them. Kaminaljuyú is a little harder to decode, however. While the presence of Teotihuacán culture is clearly

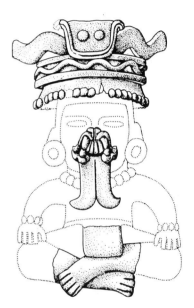

52. Zapotec ceramic figure from the state of Oaxaca.

53. Zapotec ceramic urn, Monte Albán, Oaxaca (from Willey, 1966).

113

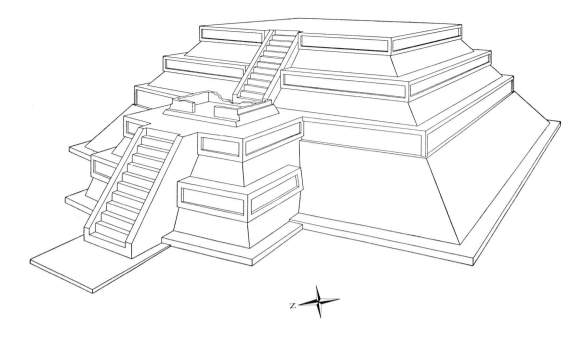

visible in the architecture of this site, there is no satisfactory explanation for it.

Be that as it may, there is undeniable evidence that Teotihuacán wielded considerable economic and religious power in the surrounding regions of Mesoamerica. But if this is indeed true, what were the conditions that led to such power? This will be discussed next.

The Social Groups

The social groups controlling Teotihuacán were the nobles and priests. Though we have no written record describing this elite, we do have archaeological data that provide insights into their activities. Many specimens of stone and clay sculpture depict gods and priests, and the priesthood likewise appears in the polychrome murals dotted about the city. It is certain that religion played a vital role in Teotihuacán, and for this reason scholars have thought that the city was governed by a theocracy, or religious group. As mentioned in the preceding chapter, it is likely that, while the priesthood wielded unequivocal power, they were supported by a number of all-important warrior chiefs. There is little doubt that the nobles exercised ideological control over the society (through the religious apparatus) and also had the necessary means of enforcement (the military apparatus). This elect group, which controlled current knowledge and technology, most likely resided in the urban complexes along the Avenue of the Dead.

Some murals feature richly dressed priests overseeing special ceremonies to invoke a good crop and soil fertility. At Tepantitla, a mural in the room adjacent to the Tlalocan Mural, shows a procession of priests, one behind the other, clad in sumptuous costumes and sporting huge headdresses adorned with long plumes. Their faces are just visible inside masks resembling crocodiles' jaws. Each priest wears earrings and a necklace, and carries a bag of seeds, which he is scattering on the ground. Emerging from his mouth is a graphic representation of speech, in this case a flowery scroll symbolizing the songs and prayers accompanying the ceremony. A similar scene is depicted in the house known as Casa Barrios, where elaborately dressed priests converge on a central feature.

Other murals concentrate on more purely symbolic aspects, such as those found in a room looking onto the Patio de los Jaguares (Jaguar Courtyard) behind the

55. Priest. Murals from the Casa Barrios at the Teopancalco site, south of Teotihuacán (from Gamio, 1922, Plate 35).

114

Palacio del Quetzalpapalotl. These murals show jaguars with shells on their back (a fertility symbol), against a red background. The animals carry elaborate headdresses of long plumes, and are blowing a shell-trumpet held in a front paw. Three drops of water are falling from the instrument. The painted border of this picture shows the face of the rain god Tlaloc inside a shell, alternated with other motifs. The scene probably represents a ceremony to invoke water deities, whose blessing was crucial for an agricultural civilization such as this.

Murals also depict warriors dressed as birds or jaguars, clearly foreshadowing the later Eagle and Jaguar warriors of the Aztec civilization. In the Casa Barrios mural, a warrior is shown fully hidden behind a mask adorned with a huge set of plumes. He is carrying a round shield and three darts held diagonally. In his right hand he is holding what might be a dart thrower.

Another highly revealing picture is the one mentioned earlier, at Tetitla, showing a kneeling figure dressed as a jaguar, holding a circular shield embellished with feathers. In his other hand, or paw, he is holding a maraca-like rattle. He is heading toward a temple along a causeway flanked by canals.

While the main focus of these murals is Teotihuacán's elite, there are glimpses of the farmers and craftsmen from the various segments of production—potters, carpenters, masons and other workers involved in constructing buildings. To give an idea of the complexity of this last particular area of production, I will list the different categories of workers participating in the construction of Teotihuacán's monuments and buildings.

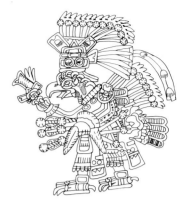

56. Eagle warrior with darts and thrower.

57. Jaguar warrior. Zacuala murals, Teotihuacán.

58. Terracotta figurines showing the clothing of the Teotihuacán aristocracy. Many show intentional skull deformation. The last two on right are high-ranking women. Museo Nacional de Antropología, Mexico City.

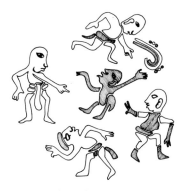

59. Commoners.
Tlalocan Mural in
Tepantitla, Teotihuacán.
Detail of lower panel.

QUARRIERS

This category of laborer quarried stone of various kinds, as the buildings were made of more than one type—one for the core of the building, another for the huge slabs that formed the panels of the *tableros*. Also an essential stone was calcareous rock (normally mined north of Teotihuacán in the Tula region).[1] This was heated to high temperatures in kilns and ground to powder to use as cement in construction work.

BUILDING WORKERS

A foreman familiar with the basics of construction led a team of builders and stonemasons, who smoothed off the exposed side of the stone blocks.

There were also carpenters and wood-choppers, as the main structure, walls and roofing required wood of different kinds. A number of laborers were also employed in such jobs as carrying rocks.

This category also included workers skilled in plastering walls and floors (using a mixture of lime and sand), who must have had expert knowledge of the consistency of the materials they were using. Once the plaster was applied, the surface was carefully sanded down, particularly the walls, which were later colored with tints (usually of mineral origin).

ARTISTS

The finishing of the building was the work of sculptors and painters. The former were highly trained in the use of stone and of their tools (chisels, slickers, etc.), which were themselves made from stone (no metal utensils were used in this particular phase of Mesoamerican history). The painters knew where to find the pigments they needed, which rocks to grind into powder, and how much binder to add to achieve the correct consistency for application to the smoothed walls. At this

60. Section of the inner core of a base.
1) Infill of *tezontle*, a volcanic rock, and *tepetate*, a rather insubstantial tufa, set in mud. 2) Fine plaster coat. 3) Mortar. 4) *Tepetate*. 5) Mortar. 6) Clay. 7) Mortar. 8) *Tepetate*. 9) River pebbles set in mud. 10) Adobe bricks. Below, the typical adobe or unbaked brick measuring approximately 21½ by 12 by 5 inches (from Gamio, 1922, Plate 16).

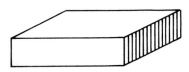

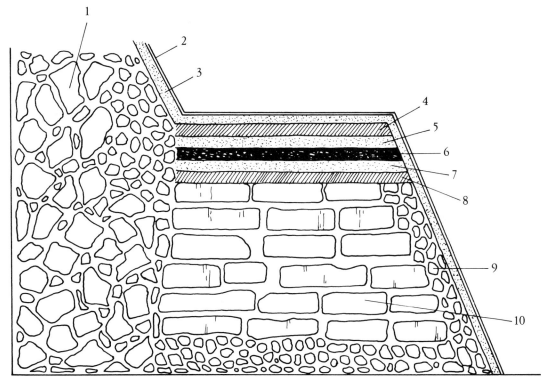

stage, one of the main influences was the complex cosmology of those who had to sketch the figures and symbols for the paintings or sculptures.

The artists directly served the ruling class, who set them to work in the decoration of their palaces and temples. In all likelihood, the training for many of these artisans and artists took place in special schools.

The murals give us a vivid picture of the common people. The Tlalocan Mural at Tepantitla, for example, portrays an assortment of people engaged in different activities. Some are tending plants, others playing or swimming in a stream. They are wearing what must have been typical dress in Teotihuacán, consisting of a simple loin-cloth. They wear neither shoes nor ornaments; hence one can assume from the simplicity of their dress that they are laborers. Some pottery also bears figures similar to those in the Tlalocan Mural.

On the subject of manual workers, it is worth noting the development of their tools and techniques. Most tool were made of stone, such as chisels, razors, knives, scrapers, and drills. Obsidian was widely used. Millon's group[2] and later investigators have established with certainty that the northern area of the city was devoted to obsidian workshops. Michael Spence[3] has estimated that, between the Miccaotli and Metepec phases, there were one hundred and five manufacturing outlets and thousands of specialists, so many in fact that an estimated six and a half percent of the population was engaged in working obsidian in some form or other.

Building required vast amounts of tools, including plumb lines and slickers for the plaster floors and walls. Some tools may well have been wooden, but so far none have been found. Wood had other important uses, however, such as the wooden planting and digging tool, the *coa*—an essential part of a farmer's equipment. Weavers, who produced fabrics of all kinds, used wooden equipment too.

As for pottery, production was prolific, and types ranged according to use. There was a simple, domestic or everyday range of wares, and there were vessels made specially for ritual purposes. The first kind shows great variety, as some vessels were apparently designed exclusively for the ruling class. Others were imported, like the Thin Orange pottery, believed to have originated in what is now the state of Puebla. George Cowgill,[4] who has analyzed the distribution of the various kinds of ware throughout the urban area, reports that remains of this particular kind of vessel (usually a thin bowl with a coil base) are more common the further one moves

61. Small terracotta head. Museo Nacional de Antropología, Mexico City.

62. Female figurine with headdress, *quezquemitl* or shawl-like blouse, and skirt. Polychrome terracotta. Museo Nacional de Antropología, Mexico City.

63. Male figurine. Semiprecious stone. Museo Nacional de Antropología, Mexico City.

64. Male figurine with headdress, loincloth and sandals. Polychrome terracotta. Museo Nacional de Antropología, Mexico City.

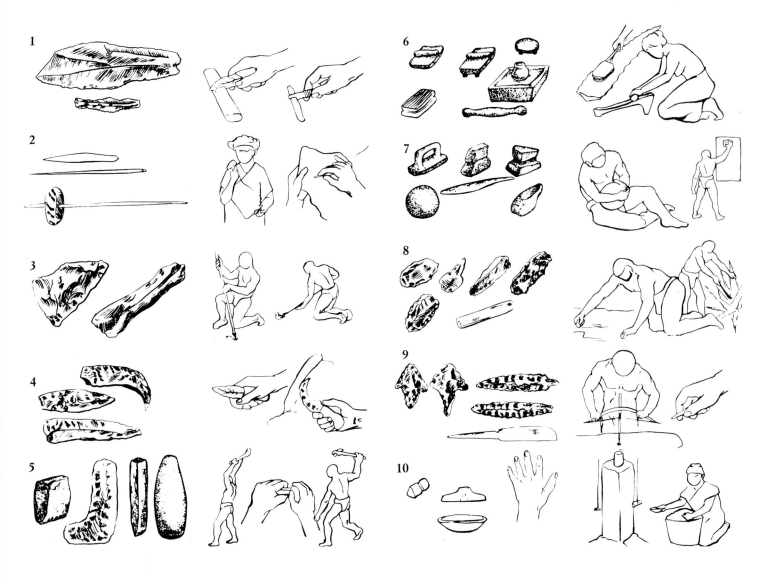

65. Tools from Teotihuacán for 1) whittling and sawing; 2) sewing and spinning; 3) digging; 4) cutting; 5) beating; 6) grinding; 7) smoothing and polishing; 8) scraping; 9) piercing; 10) measuring (from Rosa Brambila, 1986).

toward the center of Teotihuacán, indicating that the ruling class resided in the immediate vicinity of the religious precinct. However, there is also evidence of a residential complex for nobles built close to a complex for people of clearly lower rank. Much work has still to be done to resolve such queries.

Farming and Food

As explained in an earlier chapter, agriculture was a fundamental source of the city's welfare and economy. This claim is supported by such evidence as the murals with their deities and priests associated with seeds and plants. Some plants appeared regularly in the work of the Teotihuacán artists—maize, squash, beans, *nopal* (prickly pear), and tomatoes are a common sight.

Recent studies on plant remains found in numerous digs seem to corroborate the range of crops depicted in the murals. Emily McClung[5] has made a list of each variety of plant that appears:

SPECIES: *Acacia, Amaranthus, Capsicum* (red chili pepper), *Chenopodium, Cucurbita* (squash), *Lagenaria siceraria, Opuntia* (prickly pear), *Persea, Phaseolus coccineus, Phaseolus vulgaris* (bean), *Portulaca* (purslane),

Physalis (tomato), *Scirpus*, *Selaginella*, *Spondias* (plum), *Zea mays* (grains, cores, and cupule of maize).

FAMILIES: *Amaranthaceae, Cactaceae, Chenopodiaceae, Cucurbitaceae, Cyperaceae, Eleagnaceae, Graminaceae, Leguminosae, Liliaceae, Malvaceae, Solanaceae.*

FIBRES: *Ficus, Fucraea, Gossypium* (cotton), *Phragmites australis* (type of reed).

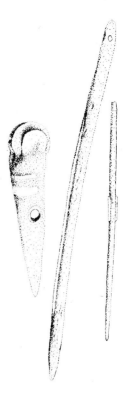

66. Bone needles. Museo Nacional de Antropología, Mexico City.

It is interesting to note that maize as a crop became less widespread in the later phases of Teotihuacán culture, while amaranth and *Chenopodium* became more popular. Focusing on the diversification of foodstuffs according to social groups, Emily McClung published a study on the Xolalpan and Metepec phases, in which she compares the remains found in Tetitla and Yayahuala. She observes that buildings in the two sites have different characteristics: Tetitla is generally more spacious and decorated walls are more common; there are also relics of ritual pottery. Yayahuala is built on a more compact plan, with no decoration and vessels of the more common type. Then she concludes that, where Tetitla has yielded a variety of food remains and seeds, finds in Yayahuala have been scarce.

Emily McClung also analyzes wildlife: in Tetitla, remains of dogs, wild game, rabbits, and an assortment of birds and rodents have been found; in Yayahuala, bird remains are more common, with traces of rodents and even hares.

All this provides a clear picture of Teotihuacán society, a society in which the various ranks were quite distinct from each other. But there is another sector of the society that deserves close study—namely, its tradesmen and the market.

67. Squash-shaped olla (from Gamio, 1922, Fig. 45).

68. Dog or coyote. Terracotta. Museo Nacional de Antropología, Mexico City.

119

69. Obsidian items.
Museo Nacional
de Antropología,
Mexico City.

In a society as complex as that of Teotihuacán, the market played a key role. It provided a hub, a focus for the exchange and barter of goods of all kinds. The market of Teotihuacán has been located in front of the Ciudadela complex, where the East-West Avenue intersects the Avenue of the Dead. Such a central position gave it unique importance in the functioning of the city.

With its vast and assorted output of goods and thriving population, Teotihuacán needed a marketplace where both home produce and wares from other regions could be bought and exchanged. Goods arrived from as far away as the Costa del Golfo, Oaxaca, and the realm of the Maya.

The presence of "foreigners" from these distant regions is of great significance. Two separate ethnic neighborhoods have been identified in Teotihuacán from remains of artifacts. One has been called the Oaxaca Quarter, the other, the Merchants' Quarter.

The first, in the western section of the city, was obviously not a prestige neighborhood. The burials, complete with funeral offerings, indicate that the inhabitants were artisans devoted to such humble occupations as the manufacture of pottery and obsidian tools. The pottery shows the marked influence of the Oaxaca style (hence the name for the neighborhood), particularly that of Monte Albán (an important town just over five hundred miles southeast of Teotihuacán, which controlled several valleys, and developed in the shadow of its powerful neighbor). Finds in the Oaxaca Quarter include burial urns from the mother town and imitation vessels in local clay. During excavations for the Proyecto Tula, Teotihuacán settlements were found outside the city, and especially to the north of the Tula region, where there were rich deposits of calcareous rock. Such settlements also showed traces of Oaxaca culture. Why did people from Oaxaca live in Teotihuacán? It may be because Oaxaca was a center for the production of dyes and pigments from the cochineal, a small insect that secretes a bright red substance, used

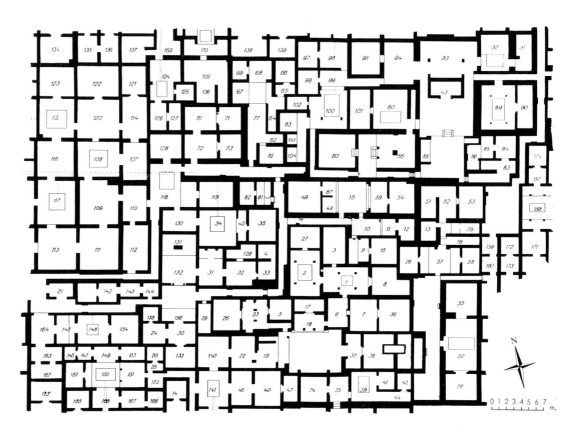

70. Plan of Tlamimilolpa,
a residential section
of Teotihuacán
(from Willey, 1966).

extensively in coloring murals. The techniques for extracting this dye were native to Oaxaca. In any event, these findings provide insights into Teotihuacán's relations with the other large towns around it.

The Merchants' Quarter had a similar connection. Located at the northwest border of the city, this neighborhood complex comprised buildings made from raw brick. René Millon[6] has suggested that it was a gathering place for the pottery produced in the Costa del Golfo. A smaller quantity of pottery came from the Maya region. On this point, Evelyn Rattray writes:

> We can safely assume that this place was inhabited by a variety of different ethnic groups. Among the imported goods, there are some local imitations. I think it very likely that this neighborhood was inhabited by the families of tradesmen originating from the Costa del Golfo. Considering the remains of the constructions, most of these people lived in small raw brick houses. It is probable that members of the aristocracy lived in the residential complex of Xocotitla, with their various relatives and entourage. Another residential complex, Tlamimilolpa, was situated at the northern side of this neighborhood, where a number of foreigners also probably lived. Maya pottery and pottery originating in the Costa del Golfo have been found in this area.[7]

It is important to grasp the great influence exercised by Teotihuacán on the entire valley and its inhabitants. The city's social and economic structure was based on a complex state-type organization, in which territory, war and trade all played a vital part, both within and without the city. This enabled Teotihuacán to control other regions and trade with most of Mesoamerica. So great was the city's influence that it was felt in Oaxaca, the Costa del Golfo, and even in the realm of the Maya.

71. Warrior with circular shield and three darts. Casa Barrios murals (from Gamio, 1922, Plate 77).

Chapter Five
RELIGION AND ART

Religion

Religion and art, which reached unprecedented heights in Teotihuacán, was a realm of symbols, a powerful sign of the mentality of the city's inhabitants.

Like most Mesoamerican peoples, the Teotihuacán people made religion a central focus of their everyday life. Each deity corresponded to a fundamental need.

But the world of the gods had its own rules, and the priesthood was the mediator through which men could consult and speak with their gods. The entire cosmology was rich in symbolism, as attested by the very orientation of the city, set majestically astride the intersection of the two vast cardinal causeways. This cosmology was directly identifiable with the city's physical environment: the Sun Pyramid, the highest building of all, was built on a grotto with an underground stream (both grottoes and water being essential features of all Pre-Hispanic cultures). The Avenue of the Dead was skewed seventeen degrees from the north-south axis to enable constant observation of the movement of the stars. This alignment determined the position of the Sun Pyramid (which faces west), the Moon Pyramid (which faces south) and other buildings, each of which had its own specific religious connotation within the Teotihuacán cosmology.

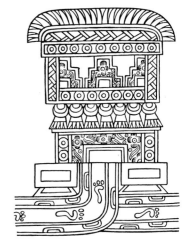

Deities and their attributes appeared everywhere in the murals and sculpture. Their likenesses were reproduced on local pottery and carved in stone.

The supreme deity of water and farming, called Tlaloc by the Aztecs, was one of the most recurrent. Other deities have turned up in the temples of Cuicuilco, such as the Old God, shown seated with a huge brazier balanced on his head. In later Mesoamerican societies, such as that of the Aztecs, this particular god, called Huehueteotl, was to become the center of the universe. Perhaps he had already attained this position in Teotihuacán, considering how often he crops up among the relics. Two other gods, both representing fertility, were the Fat God and the god of Spring, known as the skinless god or Xipe Totec. The latter appears frequently with clay heads pierced with holes for the eyes and mouth and marks representing the human skins worn by priests devoted to this particular cult worship. Then there was the water goddess, called Chalchiutlicue in Aztec times, immortalized in the huge stone statue found near the Moon Pyramid.

72. Representations of two temples. Bottom, a terracotta fragment. Top, detail from a mural in Tetitla, Teotihuacán (see Fig. 89 on page 179) (drawings by Covarrubias).

73. Tlaloc tripod vase, engraved terracotta, height 4½ inches. Museo Nacional de Antropología, Mexico City.

74. Tlaloc olla. Terracotta, height 6 inches. Museo Nacional de Antropología, Mexico City.

75. Small heads representing Xipe Totec, god of spring. Terracotta, height 1 inch. Museo Nacional de Antropología, Mexico City.

Teotihuacán people had a complex polytheist religion based on an organized form of cult worship. All the murals found so far depict religious and symbolic events, featuring deities, priests, and ritual practices.

Among others, Laurette Sejourné[1] has carried out studies on godheads such as Yacatecutli, who seems to be another manifestation of the god Tlaloc, this time representing the agricultural cycle. The god is seen scattering seeds on the ground, or carrying a basket full of corncobs, as in the Zacuala mural. Owing to the recurrence of the plumed serpent in the iconography of Teotihuacán, some scholars have insisted that Quetzalcoatl was also present in the Teotihuacán pantheon. In fact, this mythical figure belongs to a much later era.[2] As for the Templo de Quetzalcoatl in Teotihuacán's Ciudadela, Pedro Armillas states:

> On the basis of the data that has come to light, it seems certain that the temple was not consecrated to Quetzalcoatl, but to the god of rain.[3]

Román Piña Chan also comments on this issue, saying:

> In accordance with Olmec tradition, it would appear that in Teotihuacán this cult is divided into two, with one god for ground water, and another for rain, as seen in the curious figure of a snake with a rattle on its tail and quetzal feathers on the rest of its body, alluding to the running, winding course of water.[4]

The snake is also linked to the male sexual organs as a symbol of fertility. The *coa* or digging stick, used to penetrate the earth and deposit the seed, symbolizes the male sexual organ. The two terms *coa* and *coatl* (snake) have the same linguistic root, though meaning different things.

The god Tlaloc is symbolized by the serpent, bird, and jaguar. The first represents fertility; the second, a cloud bringing rainwater (beautifully illustrated in the mural in the Palacio de los Caracoles Emplumados, in which a jet of water issues from the beak of a bird and falls on a flower, perhaps meant to symbolize a specific town or place); the third, the jaguar, is probably there for his roar, like the thunder that presages the arrival of rain.

Before concluding this overview of the gods of Teotihuacán, we should mention that the later Templo Mayor in Tenochtitlan (the Aztec capital) was crowned with two smaller temples, one dedicated to Tlaloc and the other to Huitzilopochtli. Both gods were intimately linked with the race's primary needs—Tlaloc with farming, and Huitzilopochtli with war, i.e., the two pillars of Aztec economy.

One aspect of religious life in Teotihuacán has received various interpretations, namely, the question of human sacrifice. Some of the murals show priests clutching sacrificial knives, but it is by no means clear whether they are about to sacrifice humans or animals.

There are various other rites connected with rain, fertility, and so forth. For example, the mural in the Patio de los Jaguares depicts jaguars blowing shell-trumpets, presumably to bring rain, given the presence of Tlaloc in the scene. Other murals show the ceremonial dress used in these rites—the quetzal feathers, elaborate headdresses heavily decorated with ornaments, sumptuous apparel, sandals and

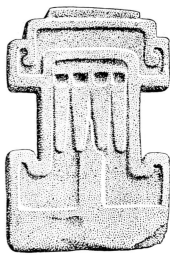

76. 77. Two images of Tlaloc in serpent form. Top, one of the stone heads that decorate the *tablero* blocks in the Templo de Quetzalcoatl.
Bottom, stylized head of the god with forked tongue, stone bas-relief, 41 inches high, found in the Superimposed Buildings. Museo Nacional de Antropología, Mexico City (drawing at bottom by Miguel Covarrubias).

78. The god Huehueteotl. Stone, height 14 inches. Museo Nacional de Antropología, Mexico City.

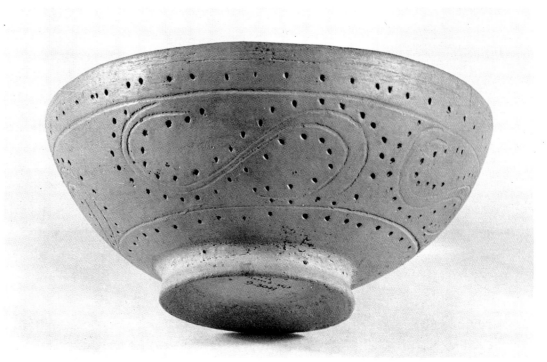

79. Offering from a burial in Teotihuacán. Engraved pottery bowl, height 4 inches. Museo Nacional de Antropología, Mexico City.

80. 81. Two representations of the jaguar, symbol of Tlaloc. Top, stone vessel, British Museum, London. Bottom, stone mask (drawings by Covarrubias).

Opposite:

41. The stone stairway of the Templo de Quetzalcoatl in the Ciudadela. Miccaotli Phase, A.D. 150-250.

Following pages:

42. A set of "talud" and "tablero" slabs in the Templo de Quetzalcoatl. "Tablero" slabs are decorated alternately with serpent heads and heads of a deity seen frontally, with the body of the serpent and various shells at intervals. "Talud" slab bears the head and the body of the serpent seen in profile.

43. A plumed serpent head on a "tablero" in the Templo de Quetzalcoatl. Everything was painted with mineral colors, faint traces of which still remain.

44. 45. Heads of deities in the Templo de Quetzalcoatl.

cloaks. Another scene shows priestesses dressed in the customary *quezquemitl* (a low-cut sleeveless blouse covering breasts and shoulders, still in use among various indigenous women), with their nails painted blue. In all probability, such rites took place on important fixed dates in the calendar (traces of which have been found at Teotihuacán).

Finally, the great number of funeral offerings and images of gods of death suggest there was a distinct cult of the dead, testifying to belief in another world.

Many myths and rites of the peoples who succeeded the Teotihuacán were drawn from the Teotihuacán legacy. A fundamental part of this legacy was the profound mystical importance of the number four, physically represented in the four quadrants of the city, the four main temples, alluding to the four cardinal points of the cosmos. Another part of the legacy was the belief that each night the sun shed its mortal flesh to descend into the nether world of the Dead (as pictured in the magnificent sculpture found in front of the Sun Pyramid). Then there were the scroll symbols representing chanting and prayers found in many murals (similar to those of the Aztecs many centuries later), and the recurrent dialogue patterns of each type of ceremony. There is much to indicate that the values held and rites practiced in Teotihuacán derived from those of the earlier cultures native to the Central Plateau before Teotihuacán was founded, and subsequently transmitted to later cultures.

Art

Every society down through the ages has expressed itself through the medium of art. The Mesoamerican civilizations have left us their vision of the universe, immortalized in color, sculpture, and architecture, a vision of symbols that vividly translates their urge for self-expression. As Paul Westheim has observed, Mesoamerican art is pervaded with a deep sense of religion, myths and beliefs.

Each of the forms of expression found in Teotihuacán has a specific language of its own, and yet the overall effect is one of truly astonishing harmony. In the Ciudadela for instance, the temple attributed to Quetzalcoatl was a vast

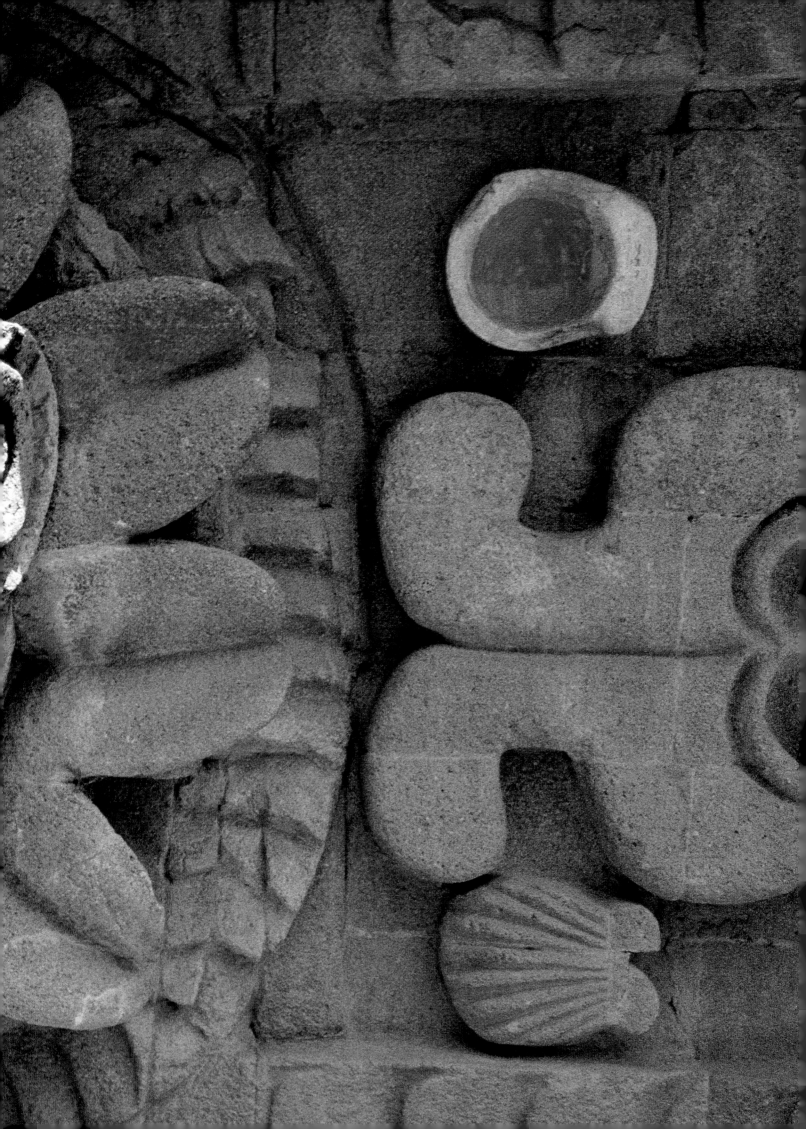

47. Northern "tablero" of the
Templo de Quetzalcoatl, with
a serpent head and heads
of a deity.

Opposite:

46. Northern "alfarda" of the
stairway up the Templo de
Quetzalcoatl, showing serpent
heads one above the other.

Following pages:

48. Serpent head at the
entrance to the Palacio del
Quetzalpapalotl or "Quetzal-
Butterfly," Xolalpan Phase,
A.D. 450-650.

49. Pillar with bas-relief of
bird seen in profile. Inner
courtyard of the Palacio del
Quetzalpapalotl.

50. Inner courtyard of the
Palacio del Quetzalpapalotl.
At left, two pillars from the

west side with bas-reliefs of
birds seen frontally. Note the
"almenas" or merlons with
the symbol of the year above
the polychrome cornice.

51. Bird head seen frontally
on a west pillar of the inner
courtyard of the Palacio del
Quetzalpapalotl.

52. Bird head seen in profile
on a pillar of the inner
courtyard of the Palacio del
Quetzalpapalotl.

*53. A plumed snail. Bas-relief
on stone with traces of
polychrome paint. Detail
from the outer facade of the
Palacio de los Caracoles
Emplumados (Tlamimilolpa
Phase, A.D. 250-450),
beneath the Palacio del
Quetzalpapalotl.*

54. Stylized snails. Mural on the plinth of the inner courtyard portico of the Palacio del Quetzalpapalotl.

56. 57. Two pumas. Details
from murals in the Patio
Blanco at Atetelco,
Teotihuacán. Xolalpan Phase,
A.D. 450-650.

Opposite:

55. Detail from a mural in
the Patio Blanco at Atetelco.

*58. 59. Details of two birds
in flight spouting water from
their beaks. Murals on the
outer base of the Palacio de
los Caracoles Emplumados.
Tlamimilolpa Phase,
A.D. 250-450.*

60. Man in water collecting
snails in a net, from Tetitla
murals, Teotihuacán.
Xolalpan Phase,
A.D. 450-650.

61. Diagrammatic
representation of buildings.
Tetitla murals.

62. Old man with beard. Tetitla murals.

63. Richly dressed deity scattering gifts on the ground. From his open hands flow jets of water containing small snails. Tetitla murals, Teotihuacán.

Following pages:

64. Detail of deity scattering gifts on the ground. Tetitla murals.

*65. Orange-colored puma
with headdress. Tetitla
murals, Teotihuacán.*

*66. Head of dog or coyote.
Tetitla murals.*

67. Bird seen frontally,
with wings outstretched.
Tetitla murals.

68. Bird seen in profile.
Tetitla murals.

69. Jaguar blowing a shell.
Mural in the Patio de los
Jaguares (Xolalpan Phase,
A.D. 450-650), behind the
Palacio del Quetzalpapalotl.

70. Head of the god Tlaloc at
the center of a shell. Detail
of mural reproduced above.

Opposite:

71. Large skull surrounded
by rays, found in front of the
Sun Pyramid. Stone with
traces of red paint. Museo
Nacional de Antropología,
Mexico City. The sculpture
symbolizes the sun
disappearing in the west
to take the light to
the world of the dead.

72. *Stylized jaguar head.*
Stone, height 31¹/₂ inches.
Museo Nacional de
Antropología, Mexico City.

73. *Skull, perhaps related to the cult of the dead, found near the Sun Pyramid. Stone, height 29 inches. Museo Nacional de Antropología, Mexico City.*

Following pages:

74. *Mask. Stone, height 7 inches. Museo Nacional de Antropología, Mexico City.*

75. *Mask. Stone encrusted with turquoise, red shell, mother-of-pearl and obsidian. Height without necklace 9½ inches. Museo Nacional de Antropología, Mexico City.*

76. *Chalchiutlicue, the water goddess, found near the Moon Pyramid. Stone, height 10 feet. Museo Nacional de Antropología, Mexico City.*

77. Composite stela used for
ball game. Found at La
Ventilla, a site southwest of
Teotihuacán. Stone, height
6¹/₂ feet. Museo Nacional de
Antropología, Mexico City.

Following pages:

78. Mask. Semiprecious
polished stone
with inlaid obsidian eyes.
Height 8 inches.
Museo del Templo Mayor,
Mexico City.

79. Detail of a vessel in the
form of an imaginary bird.
Terracotta with snail and
red-shell decorations.
Height 10 inches.
Museo Nacional de
Antropología, Mexico City.

80. 81. 82. 83. Huehueteotl,
the old fire god, a deity
originating in Cuicuilco,
represented with a brazier on
his head. Museo Nacional de
Antropología, Mexico City.

Following pages:

84. Brazier. Polychrome
terracotta, lid with molded
decoration, height 22¹/₂
inches. Museo Nacional de
Antropología, Mexico City.
Braziers of this shape,
exclusive to Teotihuacán,
were used for burning
"copal," a perfumed resin.

85. Brazier lid. Polychrome
terracotta with molded
decoration, height 10 inches.
Museo Nacional de
Antropología, Mexico City.

86. *Sculpture with unidentified motif. Stone, height 42 inches. Museo Nacional de Antropología, Mexico City.*

87. *"Almena" or merlon, with the symbol of the year. Stone, height 34¹/₂ inches. Museo Nacional de Antropología, Mexico City. Similar to those decorating the cornice of the inner courtyard of the Palacio del Quetzalpapalotl.*

Opposite:

88. *"Almena" with the head of the god Tlaloc. Terracotta, height 19¹/₂ inches. Museo Nacional de Antropología, Mexico City. Probably originally mounted on a building's roof.*

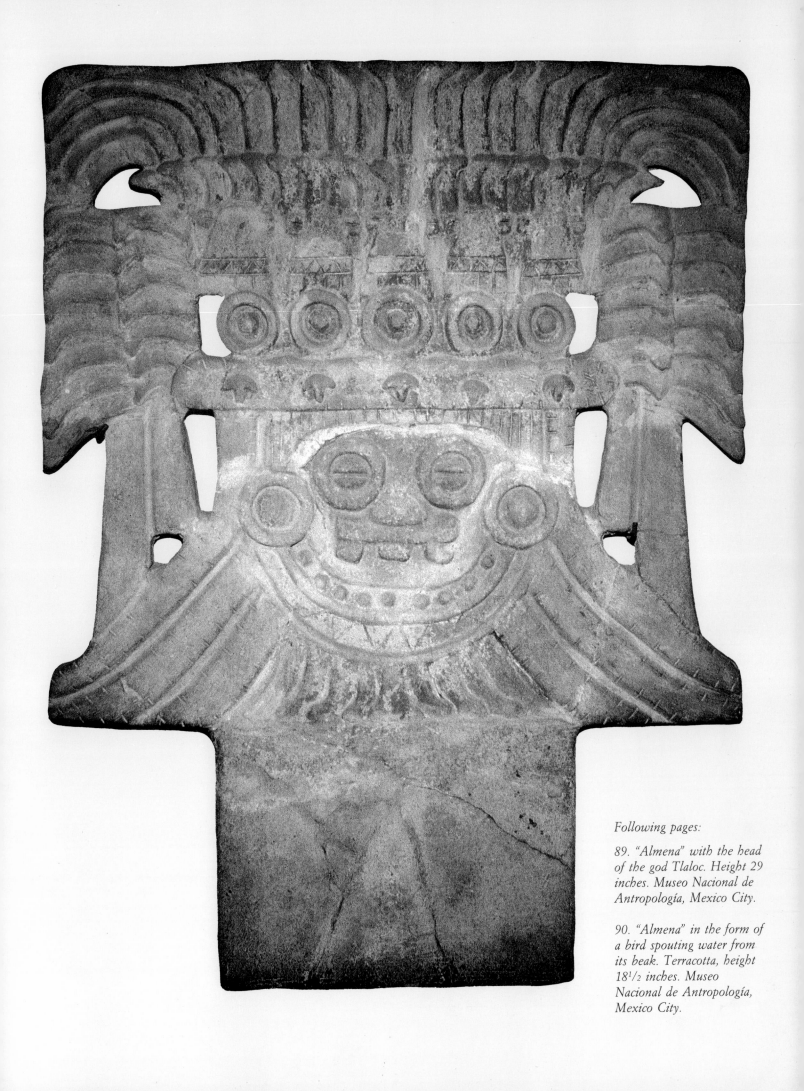

Following pages:

89. *"Almena" with the head of the god Tlaloc. Height 29 inches. Museo Nacional de Antropología, Mexico City.*

90. *"Almena" in the form of a bird spouting water from its beak. Terracotta, height 18½ inches. Museo Nacional de Antropología, Mexico City.*

91. Tripod vase.
Dark terracotta
with engraved
and modeled
decoration, height
6 inches. Museo
Nacional de
Antropología,
Mexico City.

92. *Vase with effigies of the god Tlaloc. Terracotta, height 7 inches. Museo Nacional de Antropología, Mexico City.*

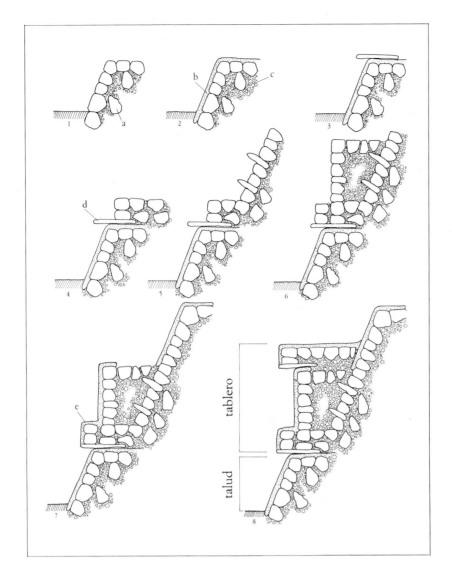

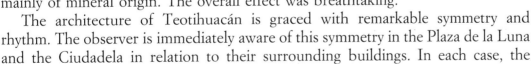

Opposite:

93. Zoomorphic "Anaranjado Delgado" pottery vessel, height 4 inches. Museo Nacional de Antropología, Mexico City.

82. Construction phases of a *talud-tablero*.
a) Infill of volcanic rock.
b) Mortar and plaster.
c) Pebbles set in mud.
d) Andesite slab to hold up the *tablero*.
e) Cornice of the *tablero*.

83. Anthropomorphic figure (top) and deity (bottom) with large headdress resembling head of owl. Terracotta figurines.

84. *Almenas* or merlons which crowned the roof of buildings.

construction of lithic slabs built on the typical Teotihuacán *talud-tablero* model. The *talud* is a sloping apron or wall on which rests a vertical slab (*tablero*) with a jutting cornice on all four sides. These slabs are overlaid to form a series of continuous shelves on a square plan. This technique was used in nearly all the buildings in Teotihuacán. In the Templo de Quetzalcoatl, the *taludes* and the *tableros* were carved with motifs—serpents, snails and shells—and punctuated by large serpent heads seemingly emerging from the *tableros*, alternated with heads of what was probably some form of water god. The whole structure was colored with dyestuffs mainly of mineral origin. The overall effect was breathtaking.

The architecture of Teotihuacán is graced with remarkable symmetry and rhythm. The observer is immediately aware of this symmetry in the Plaza de la Luna and the Ciudadela in relation to their surrounding buildings. In each case, the

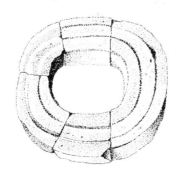

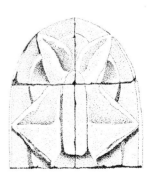

smaller buildings on either side of the main axis are equal in number. The distances between buildings were perfectly judged. In the Plaza de la Luna, we find three buildings on the west side of the central axis, balanced by three others on the east. The central building on each side is set slightly in front of the two flanking it, and the resulting effect is one of great harmony on both horizontal and vertical planes.

PAINTING

Although in most areas explored so far little or no sculpture has been found integrated with the architecture, the temples, palaces and houses were nearly always decorated with murals, usually of a symbolic nature. The most common color was red—often used as a background—with green, yellow, orange, blue, white, and black to depict the details.

The handiwork of Teotihuacán's painters expresses the same innate harmony found in the architecture. In a typical room, the door is set in the center of the wall,

85. Water deity with two assistants, upper panel of the Tlalocan Mural at Tepantitla, Teotihuacán. Replica, Museo Nacional de Antropología, Mexico City.

86. Scenes from earthly life, lower panel of the Tlalocan Mural at Tepantitla, Teotihuacán. Replica, Museo Nacional de Antropología, Mexico City (see Plate 29).

and on either side, murals carry a set of symmetrical running motifs, which generally converge on the doorway. There are some exceptions however, as in the Tepantitla mural, where the scene on one side does not correspond to its counterpart.

Examples of murals found in Tepantitla are, generally speaking, of outstanding importance. It is worth our looking at them more closely at this point. Let us first consider the Tlalocan Mural on the east side of Tepantitla. This mural is a remarkable series of painted decorations extending the length of the four inside walls of a room. The mural is split into two panels, one above the other, with two distinct subjects: the upper panel depicts the deities, and the lower shows earthly scenes of games and festivities.

In the bottom right corner of the lower panel, a figure shedding two tears and crowned with a branch is singing (symbolized by the scroll issuing from his mouth). Beneath him a spring (with a frog perched in the center?) disgorges a long stream, irrigating a series of cultivated fields and filling other fountains on its way. Below the stream a set of small rectangles denote *chinampas*, in green and blue, complete with crops of flowers and fruit. The water flows left and then curves down toward the bottom before rising into a kind of pyramid of waves in which some figures are seen swimming and playing.

Above the stream, against a dark red background, are a host of other small human figures interspersed with insect or plant motifs. The figures depicted are engaged in various activities: some carry others on their shoulders, in what seems like some kind of race; others are squatting down one behind the other, each with a hand between his legs to grip the hand of the person behind; in another corner, a male figure is sitting cross-legged, weaving flowers together and adorning himself with his work. Four other figures carrying branches seem to be chasing a butterfly, while yet another four are holding a man by his arms and feet, most likely playing at tossing him in the air. On the left there is a figure with a ball lying before him. In addition to these scenes of action, there are various other motifs, featuring butterflies and a dragonfly. There is no doubt that the mural depicts people enjoying themselves near the cultivated fields. Each of the figures is barefoot and wears only a *maxtlatl* or loin-cloth, with no ornaments. Clearly these people were of low social rank, perhaps peasants, celebrating the harvest or some other event. It has been suggested that the scene shows Tlalocan, the paradise home of the god Tlaloc and the destination of all those who died by drowning.

The upper panel of the mural portrays a celestial scene. A large central figure depicting a god of harvests (Tlaloc), dominates the scene. Beside him one can see two Tlaloques (assistants to the water god), and below him the place where he keeps the seeds of various plants. With its farming theme, flowering plants and cultivated fields, this mural is an outstanding celebration of the basic needs of the people who

87. Detail of the mural in the Templo de los Animales Mitológicos, on the west side of the Avenue of the Dead. Replica, Museo Nacional de Antropología, Mexico City.

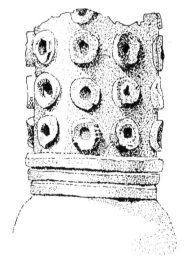

88. Fragment of column adorned with relief rings. Stone with remains of red paint, diameter 15 inches. Museo Nacional de Antropología, Mexico City.

89. Figure dressed as a jaguar heading toward a temple. Murals at Tetitla, Teotihuacán.

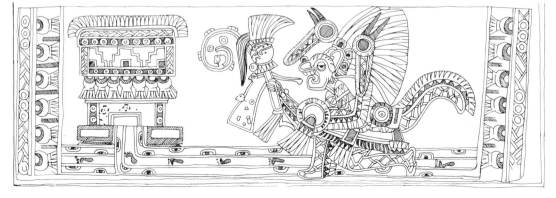

90. Detail of murals in the
Templo de la Agricultura,
on the west side of the
Avenue of the Dead.
Replica, Museo Nacional de
Antropología, Mexico City.

created it. The anonymous Teotihuacán artist or artists who painted the mural showed remarkable ability in depicting all these individual scenes and details, particularly in delineating the smaller human figures, which are never more than two inches high. The red background makes the elements stand out clearly, be they people or insects, or streams painted in yellows, blues and greens.

Another striking example of the artists' skill in painting miniature figures is the mural in the Templo de los Animales Mitológicos, which shows fish, jaguars, and other symbolic life-forms.

The murals in Teotihuacán cover a variety of themes, but all have a significant symbolic content. In the Tetitla residential complex there are outstanding murals, such as the one of a man standing waist-deep in water, holding a net in which he is gathering snails of some kind. Another mural of astonishing beauty pictures a bird with outstretched wings. Sometimes the whole animal is shown, sometimes only the head. In the vestibule of one of the rooms looking onto the courtyard, there is a mural showing orange pumas which converge inward from the side walls toward the entrance. The finer details of the bird and pumas have been captured with great skill.

Two other paintings in the Tetitla complex deserve mention. The first, in the vestibule facing the pumas mural, on the opposite side of the courtyard, portrays a richly dressed deity with arms outstretched, scattering gifts on the ground. Among these we can make out small animal heads and snails. The second mural, close to the vestibule, portrays a figure on his way to a temple, dressed as a jaguar, as described earlier. He is on one knee and is completely covered by the animal hide. The figure's head is adorned with an impressive crown of feathers. In his left hand he carries a shield, in his right what must be some kind of rattle which, given the typical scrolling lines coming out of it, is making a sound. He is heading toward a temple along a causeway flanked by two canals. The *talud-tablero* base of the temple is crowned with a chamber with a doorway. The rather complex design of the roof with its *almenas* (merlons) is typical of Teotihuacán architecture. Footprints have been drawn along the path to show the direction in which the figure is heading. Here again, the mural depicts ritual activity which we are as yet unable to decipher.

However, this mural provides us with another example of the kind of symbology present in the complex art of Teotihuacán.

In other areas of the capital, we find that the murals are adapted to their particular environment. In the Avenue of the Dead, for instance, there are large-scale murals (nine to twelve feet wide) matching the dimensions of this imposing causeway (thirty-five to fifty-five feet wide). Visitors can thus take in the entire scene represented in the mural. This also applies to the murals in the Templo de la Agricultura and to others which, regrettably, have been almost completely erased. Similarly, the mural depicting a huge jaguar against a background of diagonal bands, mentioned in Chapter two, also belongs to this category.

In conclusion, it is important to acknowledge the great number of other pictorial decorations found elsewhere in and on the city's buildings. This astonishing world of color transcends mere form and introduces us to symbolic entities that narrate the life of a population deeply tied to nature and the mysteries of ritual.

SCULPTURE

The stone sculptures of Teotihuacán can be divided into two groups: those that form an integral part of the architecture, usually of large dimensions, and the smaller sculptures, which include masks and several figures representing Huehueteotl, animals and other subjects. One sculpture in particular is quite unique, namely, the massive stone figure representing Chalchiutlicue, a female deity related to water worship. The piece is ten feet tall and five feet wide. As mentioned earlier, the statue was unearthed near the Moon Pyramid and is perhaps the only one of this size within the perimeter of the city. It is currently on display at the Museo Nacional de Antropología.

On examples of sculpture integrated with the architecture, we have already discussed the Templo de Quetzalcoatl, which offers the most elaborate range of this kind of sculpture. The building, which is constructed from perfectly interlocking blocks of stone, is graced with extraordinary harmony and rhythm. The many figures adorning it are proof of the skill of the sculptors involved in its construction. The Templo is a superb example of architecture blended with sculpture and painted decoration. Its architects clearly possessed not only the ability necessary for realizing such an elaborate project, but also such a profound sense of the symbols and myths of their culture that they were able to translate them physically into the stone—the sculptures are so imbued with symbology that they completely transcend form and seem virtually empowered to speak.

Sculpture was a vital feature in other Teotihuacán temples, though it never quite reaches the heights of expression found in the Templo de Quetzalcoatl.

Among the sculptures of larger dimensions integrated with the architecture is a stone disk with a human skull carved at its center, surrounded by rays that still show traces of red pigment. It was found in the plaza in front of the Sun Pyramid. It is thought to represent the setting sun, which disappeared in the west to take the light to the world of the dead. The skull is seen frontally on both sides of the sculpture.

The access ramp to the Palacio del Quetzalpapalotl, situated at the southwest corner of the square in front of the Moon Pyramid, and the superbly crafted pillars adorning the main courtyard are of particular note. The ramp is embellished with a large serpent head whose jaw was sculpted separately and added later. The square courtyard has four pillars on each side bearing bas-relief sculptures of birds seen in profile. In the pillars on the west side the birds are sculpted frontally, as if to underline the great importance the direction of the setting sun had for the

92. Stone mask (from Willey, 1966).

93. Typical Teotihuacán mask. Circa A.D. 500. Semiprecious stone, height 6 inches. Museo Nacional de Antropología, Mexico City.

Teotihuacán. The pillars still show traces of the original red, green and yellow pigments with which they were decorated.

Beneath the Palacio del Quetzalpapalotl (and completely covered by it) is the Palacio de los Caracoles Emplumados. It was given this name because the outside of the main facade is set with four vertical bands of stone, each one decorated with two huge *caracoles emplumados* or plumed snails in bas-relief, with traces of green and red pigment. The two jutting corners of this facade are sculpted with four-petaled flowers painted yellow and red.

Another sculpture that has a specific function is the Stela de La Ventilla, a complex situated southwest of Teotihuacán. The stela is magnificently crafted and served as a "goalpost" in the local ball game which was practiced outdoors in Teotihuacán, with posts of this kind placed at either end of the pitch. Part of the Tepantitla Mural shows such posts, and figures playing ball with a form of stick or bat.

Generally speaking, the stone sculptures from Teotihuacán frequently portray figures of deities or sacred animals, such as the serpent.

The individual sculptures not integrated with the buildings include some pieces of great artistic merit. There are masks carved in semiprecious stone, some incrusted with shells or obsidian to mark the eyes and teeth. All of them are fashioned in the typical Teotihuacán triangular shape. There are also whole human and animal figures. The artists who sculpted the stone were remarkably skilled, because they worked with stone and abrasive instruments to gradually smooth the stone to the desired shape. Various kinds of stone were used, including obsidian, slate, alabaster, and greenstone. Some were readily available in the Teotihuacán Valley, the rest were imported from outlying regions.

POTTERY

Many pieces of Teotihuacán pottery also reached high levels of perfection. Some were decorated with colors, applied with astonishing delicacy and expertise, testimony to the great skill of the city's artists.

The pottery shows considerable variety both in form and function. One of the more characteristic types is the *florero* jar with bowed base and high narrow neck, usually in dark colors tending toward black. Equally characteristic are the plates with tiny round feet known as *soportes-botón*. These too were generally dark in color. There was also another very particular variety of vessel, fashioned from orange-colored clay. This was known as *barro Anaranjado Delgado* (Thin Orange pottery). Specimens of exceptional quality include the large coil-based bowls. This kind of ware appears to have been manufactured in the area that is now the state of Puebla, which was most likely under the control of Teotihuacán.

Special mention should also be made of those vessels in which the painted decorations have created clay works of art of exceptional quality. Generally, after being fired, the vases were layered with fine stucco onto which colors were later applied in either fresco or tempera technique. The motifs vary but are always symbolic.

Another interesting type of vessel, exclusive to Teotihuacán, is the pottery brazier. This receptacle was used for burning *copal*, a form of Pre-Hispanic incense. It was fitted with a large elaborate lid with a human face in the center surrounded by ornamental motifs. It is important to remember that these decorations—butterflies, circles or other motifs—were created separately with molds and then applied to the lid. Braziers of this type are peculiar to this culture and cannot be traced in any cultures preceding that of Teotihuacán.

It is essential to mention also the vast output of human figurines and pottery deities, usually made from molds. Excavations in the Cuadrángulo Norte close to the Ciudadela have yielded clay molds for producing figurines in series (see

94. Olla with three handles. Terracotta, height 7 inches. Museo Nacional de Antropología, Mexico City. One or both the upper handles served for holding the receptacle, the lower one for pouring.

95. Tripod vase with slab-shaped legs. Terracotta with traces of fresco decoration, height 6 inches. Museo Nacional de Antropología, Mexico City. As in Figure 96, the cylinder base is encircled with rattles made from hollow spheres with a slit, each containing a small terracotta ball.

96. Fragment of a tripod vase depicting a figure beneath a cacao plant; a quetzal bird is perched in a branch overhead. Terracotta, height 4 inches.

97. Upper part of brazier lid. Polychrome ceramic with molded decorations.

98. *Florero* jar. Dark terracotta, height 4 inches. Museo Nacional de Antropología, Mexico City.

99. Cylindrical tripod vessel with lid. Engraved terracotta, height 11 inches.

Appendix). Among the most frequent are the very simple, small unadorned heads that have turned up throughout the urban area. Figures of deities such as Xipe and the Fat God are equally common. Xipe is easily recognized from the three holes representing his eyes and mouth.

The evidence suggests that, in Teotihuacán, pottery production was well-established, and there is no doubt that a sizable number of people were involved, given the vast quantities of fragments that have turned up during surveying and excavation within the city's perimeter. Of course, pottery remains are of vital assistance to archaeologists, as they enable them to understand the people under study, their technology and hence their ability to fashion and fire clay, their possible commercial links, the representations of their gods, the ornamentation they used and the kind of plants and animals around them. Furthermore, pottery has enabled archaeologists to apply dates to relics and cultures. It also conveys how a given people expressed themselves through clay, establishing a valid art form.

100. Female figurine. Polychrome terracotta. Museo Nacional de Antropología, Mexico City.

101. Female figurine with feathered headdress, from La Ventilla, Teotihuacán. Terracotta. Museo Nacional de Antropología, Mexico City.

Conclusions

Documentation on other art forms, such as music, dancing and poetry is not forthcoming. Some musical instruments have survived, however, such as flutes and terracotta flageolets. Shells were also used as musical instruments on occasion. What we cannot tell is what kind of music the Teotihuacán enjoyed, as there are no written records to document it. Regrettably, also, while we have considerable information on Aztec dance and poetry forms, both directly and indirectly, data on these cultural aspects of Teotihuacán are so far absent, except for a mural in Atetelco depicting a warrior dancing on a small temple, with footprints indicating the dance steps.

However, we do know that styles popular in Teotihuacán spread to the surrounding regions and influenced their art. Many sites bear Teotihuacán symbols, such as Cacaxtla in the state of Tlaxcala where, despite local hostility toward Teotihuacán, the inhabitants (the Olmec-Xicalanca) painted numerous murals in

102. Decorative motifs from clay molds created for producing ceramics in series (from Gamio, 1922, Plate 118).

103. Panpipes. Terracotta, height 2 inches. Museo Nacional de Antropología, Mexico City.

104. Warrior dancing, as suggested by footsteps. Atetelco murals, Teotihuacán.

Teotihuacán style. These murals narrate a terrifying battle between one group of figures dressed as birds and another dressed as jaguars. The bird-warriors have Maya characteristics, and the jaguar-warriors represent the peoples of the Central Plateau. The latter army is victorious in the end. The battle-scene is powerfully rhythmic, almost like a dance of death. The jaguar-warriors throw themselves on their enemies, their faces contorted with fierce loathing. Their spears and shields form a single line that metes out death. In contrast, the bird-warriors lie on the ground, wounded or slain. They are a picture of defeat. One of them is trying to tear out the head of an arrow from his cheek; another, stretched out on the ground, vainly tries to stuff his innards back into a horrible gash in his belly. The mural is accepted as dating from the year A.D. 650, a century before the fall of Teotihuacán, and is proof that at that time (and perhaps before) war was a crucial instrument in economic and military expansion. The Teotihuacán must surely have been hostile to the people of Cacaxtla. Thus, the art of the Teotihuacán's contemporaries provide us with some vital insights into their history. Besides its artistic merits, this mural enables us to grasp the needs and problems of the people living on the fringes of the awesome empire that Teotihuacán had built for itself, a city that was the very symbol of domination and power.

105. Dancing figurine. Terracotta. Museo Nacional de Antropología, Mexico City.

Appendix
RECENT ARCHAEOLOGICAL DISCOVERIES IN TEOTIHUACÁN
(1980-1988)

by Rubén Cabrera Castro

Since 1980 Teotihuacán has been the object of a series of important archaeological inquiries. One of the leading studies is the Proyecto Arqueológico Teotihuacán, which the Instituto Nacional de Antropología has initiated at various points in the city, especially in the Ciudadela and along the Avenue of the Dead. In this Appendix, the new inquiries will be discussed by the archaeologist Rubén Cabrera Castro. The latest excavations have certainly increased hopes for a deeper knowledge of the vast city. Meanwhile, excavation work continues, and each day Teotihuacán reveals more of the history it had hidden for so many centuries.

EDUARDO MATOS MOCTEZUMA

Proyecto Arqueológico Teotihuacán
and Proyecto Templo de Quetzalcoatl

The recent archaeological operations in Teotihuacán have brought previously uncharted areas to light and uncovered new relics to complement the many finds already explored and studied. Such finds enable the daily stream of visitors to acquire a more complete understanding of the various architectural complexes of the vast city which, in its time, was the most important in the whole of the American continent.

The Proyecto Arqueológico Teotihuacán (or Proyecto 80-82), sponsored by the Mexican government from 1980 to 1982, assembled a considerable quantity of new data, much of which is still being analyzed. This information has broadened our knowledge of Teotihuacán culture and consolidated certain ideas on the population's social and cultural development. But some of the finds are completely new and have generated ideas and postulates that will inevitably be confirmed or rectified by future discoveries.

The Proyecto 80-82, which involved social research into the ancient heart of the city, also drew on studies whose themes had been of little interest to previous inquiries. It dealt with issues more closely tied to the city's infrastructure: its farming, various neighborhoods and manufacturing centers, rural population, and interaction with outside cultures. Also considered were scientific questions, such as Teotihuacán astronomy, its calendar and methods of calculation. Inquiries were opened on funeral rites and the general chronology and sequence of Teotihuacán pottery. The discovery of the large architectural complex in the center of the old city has also provided data, particularly on urban planning and layout and, of course, on the architecture itself. Vital new information has emerged on the religious practices, politics and ideas of the Teotihuacán people.

We should point out that the excavations carried out as part of Proyecto 80-82 did not only involve the last and most recent phase of construction. By exploring deeper layers at appropriate points of the site, the Proyecto identified entire sequences of various phases of construction. The material unearthed has also enabled a more accurate dating of the phases of Teotihuacán culture.

106. Area of recent
excavation campaigns in the
ceremonial precinct of
Teotihuacán.

CIUDADELA

1B'. Structure of small superimposed
    temples
1C', 1D, 1E. Conjuntos
    Habitacionales or residential
    complexes
2. North, east and south sections of
    the Gran Plataforma or raised
    platform enclosing the Ciudadela
3. West section of the Gran
    Plataforma with access to
    Ciudadela
4. Fifteen pyramidal bases (or
    secondary temples)
5. Templo de Quetzalcoatl
6. Building with four *talud-tablero*
    sections which covered the Templo
    de Quetzalcoatl
7. Explanada or clearing (Plaza 2)
8. Cuadrángulo Norte
9. Avenue of the Dead
10. San Juan River

COMPLEXES WEST OF
THE AVENUE OF THE DEAD

11. Northwest Complex of the San
    Juan river
12. Superimposed Buildings
13. West Plaza Complex of the
    Avenue of the Dead

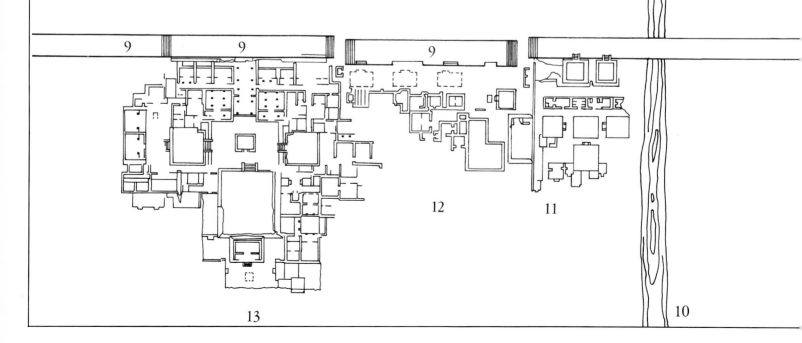

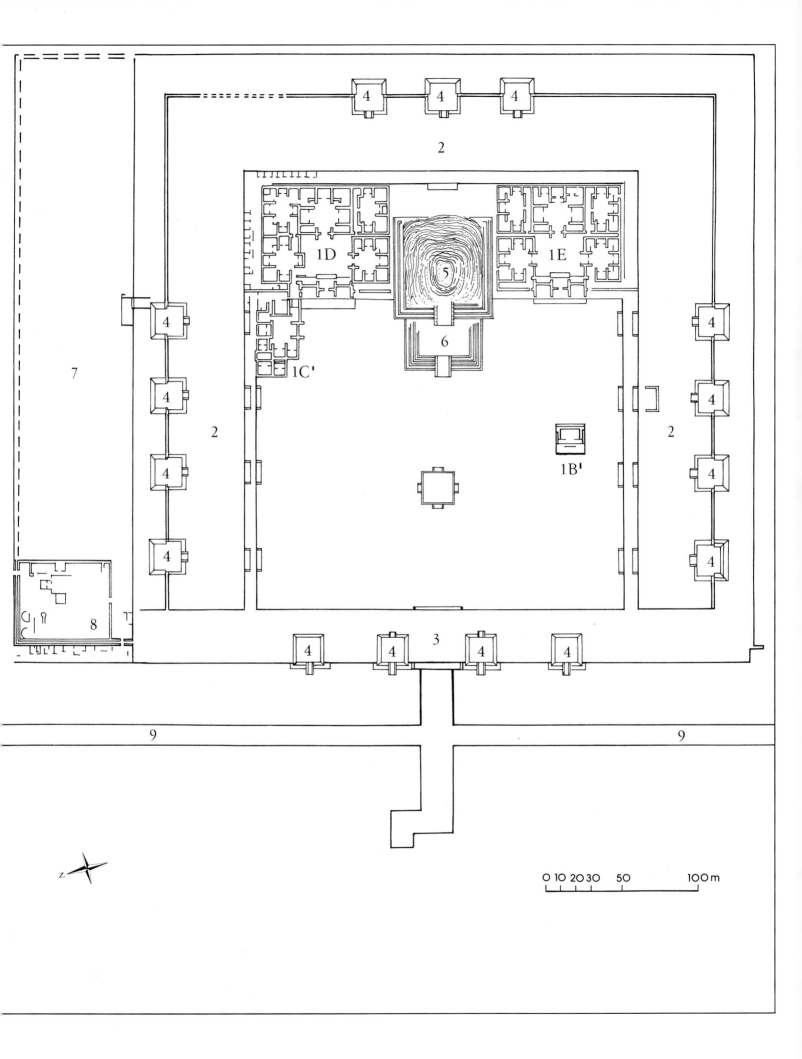

Here we will be taking a general view of the many new finds that have emerged from Proyecto 80-82 and successive research projects, as well as from the latest digs carried out under the recent Proyecto Templo de Quetzalcoatl research program, which began in 1988 and is currently ending the second stage of excavations.

The Ciudadela

This vast complex covers a surface area of 133,000 square yards. The area contains three large residential enclosures and eighteen pyramidal bases, including the magnificent Templo de Quetzalcoatl, which rises in the center of a broad *explanada* or clearing completely enclosed by four huge raised platforms, each one having on top four small pyramid bases, except the east platform, which has three.

In the past, the Ciudadela has been investigated in numerous research programs. The most important, in terms of the extension of the archaeological digs carried out, was the study directed by Manuel Gamio[1] from 1917 to 1922, during which over sixty percent of the buildings of the Ciudadela were brought to light.

The Proyecto Arqueológico Teotihuacán 80-82 unearthed additional sections of this enormous complex. At present, all that remains to be excavated is a very small section of the rear, after which we will be able to admire the Ciudadela as it was during the last phase of occupation.

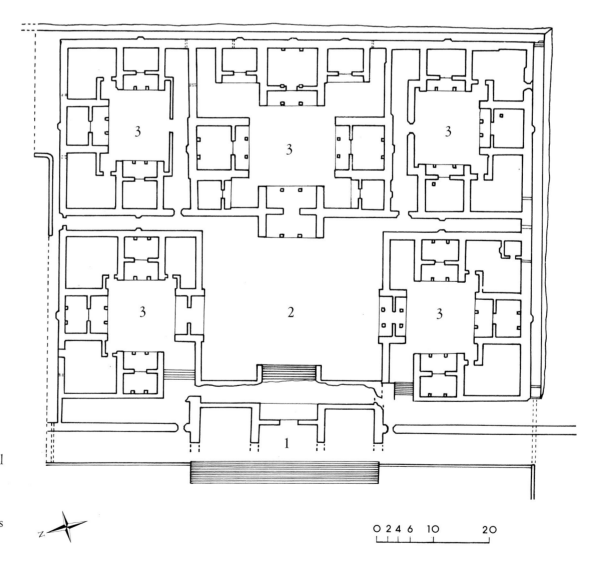

107. Plan of the Conjunto Habitacional 1E, south of the Templo de Quetzalcoatl in the Ciudadela.
1. Access stairway
2. Central plaza
3. Courtyards of the various sections

94. The west stairway in the central courtyard of the West Plaza Complex of the Avenue of the Dead as it stands today: the photograph shows only the later construction phase, with one surviving jaguar head along the "alfarda" or sloping ramp.

95. The same stairway during the excavation work conducted by the Proyecto Arqueológico Teotihuacán 1980-82: the underlying earlier construction phase is also visible, showing two serpent heads with forked tongues—in better repair than those from the later phase because they were protected under a layer of infill.

Following pages:

96. Central courtyard of the West Plaza Complex. The west stairway, with the jaguar head, is at the left. In the background, the Sun Pyramid.

97. West stairway of the
central courtyard of the West
Plaza Complex of the Avenue
of the Dead.

Following pages:

98. Large jaguar stone
head. West stairway of the
central courtyard of the
West Plaza Complex, seen in
the later construction phase
(see Plate 94).

99. Serpent head with forked
tongue. Large monolithic
sculpture with traces of
polychrome paint. It shows
the typical traits of the
plumed serpent, together
with feline and
anthropomorphic features.
West stairway of the West
Plaza Complex, earlier
construction phase
(see Plate 95).

Opposite:

100. *Representation of Tlaloc. Fragment of a large carved frieze made up of several joined stone slabs. It was found in the West Plaza Complex of the Avenue of the Dead. Museo Arqueológico de Teotihuacán.*

101. *Tripod vase with openwork supports in the form of "almenas." The scrolls and scribbles decoration is typical of El Tajín ware.*

102. *Female figure with "quezquemitl" or shawl-shaped blouse. Engraved polished serpentine. Found in the West Plaza Complex of the Avenue of the Dead.*

Following pages:

103. *Central courtyard of the West Plaza Complex of the Avenue of the Dead.*

104. *Northwest Complex of the San Juan river. In background at right, the Ciudadela. This recently excavated residential complex is situated at the corner where the river crosses the west side of the Avenue of the Dead.*

105. 106. Northwest
Complex of the San
Juan river.

107. Northwest Complex of
the San Juan river.

108. Structure with remains
of decorated plaster.
Northwest Complex of the
San Juan river.

109. Tripod cylinder jar with slab-shaped supports. Fresco-painted decoration with flowers and fruit.

108. View of the Conjunto Habitacional 1D from the summit of the Templo de Quetzalcoatl. Note the large central plaza surrounded by residential sections. In the background, the Sun Pyramid.

THE CONJUNTOS HABITACIONALES 1D AND 1E

Along the north and south sides of the Templo de Quetzalcoatl, symmetrically on either side of the east-west axis of the Ciudadela, there are two large residential complexes, called Conjunto 1D and Conjunto 1E. These were only partly excavated during Gamio's 1917-1922 study and it was not until the Proyecto 80-82 that both complexes were exposed in their entirety. The two *conjuntos*, each of which covers an area of 6,790 square feet, are of exceptional design. Both are aligned with secondary symmetrical axes and have a similar plan of access points, pathways and distribution of space, particularly with regard to the symmetry of their layout, the extent of covered and open spaces, and the function served by some of these spaces.

Each complex is bordered at north, east and south by tall protective walls, cut through with narrow secondary points of access. On the west the complexes are bordered by raised platforms crowned with various chambers from which the main access route was controlled. This is linked to the large internal *explanada* or clearing of the Ciudadela by a flight of steps. Each complex is split up into five sections, linked by passageways and courtyards, with a large central plaza, the focal point of the structure.

As yet there is no precise data on the function of these complexes. But various examples of *almenas* (merlons) have been found here and there, together with defense walls complete with checkpoints. The complexes are closely linked with the Templo de Quetzalcoatl and (as we shall see later) with a specialized pottery workshop. These features indicate that they were the focus of the administration and part of a larger government precinct, the Ciudadela itself.

THE CONJUNTO HABITACIONAL 1C'

When, toward the end of Phase III, the population of Teotihuacán was at its peak, Conjunto 1D had to expand. A residential unit was therefore built to its west side, which has been called Conjunto Habitacional 1C'.[2] This complex, most of which

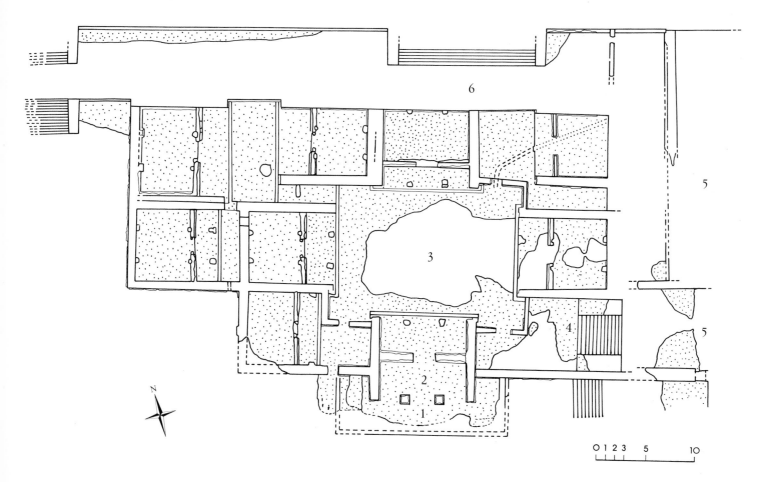

109. Plan of the Conjunto
Habitacional 1C' north of
the Templo de Quetzalcoatl
in the Ciudadela.
1. Main access
2. Porticoed platform
3. Central courtyard
4. Access stairway to
Complex 1D
5. Complex 1D
6. North section of the Gran
Plataforma, inside

was unearthed during the 1980-1982 project, is situated at the north side of the
explanada in the Ciudadela, and is directly linked to Conjunto 1D.

At first, communication between the two complexes was through a corridor or
passage with plaster walls and, later, by a set of steps serving both complexes.
Access from the *explanada* to Conjunto C1' was through a large porticoed platform,
whose flat roof was supported by heavy side walls and massive pillars covered with a
thick layer of red-painted plaster. Beyond the portico was a spacious central
courtyard, bordered on the other three sides by similar covered porticoes. From the
central courtyard, which served as the hub of the complex, narrow passageways led
to other sections or groups of rooms, arranged around smaller secondary courtyards
from which they drew the necessary daylight. The roofing of these rooms and the
porticoed areas were decorated with *almenas* and other features depicting Tlaloc,
the water god.

THE GRAN PLATAFORMA

The exterior section of the Gran Plataforma or raised platform enclosing the
Ciudadela has recently been closely investigated in its north, south and east sides,
revealing the Plataforma's true dimensions, form, surviving sections and the
techniques used in its construction. The inner core of the Plataforma is made up
either of *adobes* (square sun-dried bricks) carefully arranged in *cajones* (compact
blocks), or of rubble set in mud. This core is covered with high stone *talud* walls that
provide an impenetrable barrier, clad on the outside with a thick layer of mortar.
The surface of the mortar reveals remains of white, green and yellow painted motifs
bordered in black, all against a red background. It would appear that this massive
talud was originally decorated with large-scale murals.

Thanks to the depth to which the excavations have been taken, three

210

superimposed layers of construction have been found in the Plataforma, together with a series of rooms aligned one behind the other, with small cisterns along the porticoes for collecting rainwater, some linked by gutters.

Arranged in splendid symmetry on the upper section of the Gran Plataforma are fifteen pyramidal bases known as the *templos secundarios* or secondary temples. Though less imposing than the Templo de Quetzalcoatl, these temple bases are larger than Edificio 1B' (detailed later). Some of these bases were originally discovered during Gamio's 1917-1922 excavations, though no further investigations were made at the time. During the deeper excavations conducted for the Proyecto 80-82, older constructions were found in their midst which had been covered over by the later ones.

THE EDIFICIO 1B'

The exploration of Edificio 1B' has yielded some surprises. The building is situated at the southern side of the Ciudadela *explanada* or clearing, and comprises a set of small temples built one over the other, the most recent having been unearthed during Gamio's 1917-1922 project. In order to learn more about the building, excavations were made at its center, which soon revealed the existence of older structures below it. The digs were conducted further to study the various phases of the building's construction, which were found to comprise seven levels containing the entire history of Teotihuacán, from its origins to its decline.

The inner layers of Edificio 1B' belong to a phase which we have called "pre-Ciudadela," i.e. predating the construction of the Ciudadela itself.[3] The *explanada* comprises many structures belonging to this phase, later demolished or built over.

Some of the floors found in Edificio 1B' are in good condition because they were deliberately spared destruction during subsequent phases of construction. One of these floors bears scroll patterns and geometric motifs in dark red against a light red background. So far in Teotihuacán no other examples of this style of art have been found. The designs attest to cultural links with the regions of the Mexican Gulf.

On a small platform above these floors (which probably formed part of precincts that no longer exist) there is a complete temple in typical Teotihuacán style, terminating at one end in *talud* walling.

Proceeding upward, we find a base with a high *talud-tablero* wall encircling the temple of the preceding period. In this case, however, the *tablero* differs in style from those normally used in Teotihuacán. Instead of being bordered by wide moldings on all four sides, it is framed by a surface set slightly higher than the *talud* and has moldings on the other three sides. Like the building below it, this one is facing west, with steps and *alfardas* (ramps) on each side painted with concentric black and green circles against a red background. These symbolic patterns are fairly recurrent in Teotihuacán imagery. The *taludes* and *tableros* on the four sides of the building were also decorated with painted designs. Decorations on the *tableros* are in better condition than those on the *taludes*, and some bear symbols from the Teotihuacán calendar, painted in red, green and black. The base was once crowned with a temple, of which only part of the raised section has been recovered.

In the next layer up there is another pyramidal base. Despite its state of decay, there is sufficient data to confirm that this construction had *talud-tablero* walls typical of Teotihuacán architecture.

Next we find a building that encases all the preceding structures. This too is a pyramidal base formed from a single unit built with *talud* walls and, like the structures below, it faces west. Some remains of the foundations and the original raised sections of the temple have survived. This construction was the one unearthed in Gamio's 1917-1922 campaign, before the entire Ciudadela area was reinvestigated during the Proyecto 80-82.

The Templo de Quetzalcoatl

The most important information on Teotihuacán comes from this colossal monument, which is the largest and most significantly positioned building in the entire Ciudadela complex.

Attempts were made to sketch the original form of the monument on the basis of data from previous investigations. It was thought to have a square plan, with six stepped sections. In view of the number of colossal heads still adorning the steps of the temple's west face, it was presumed that these heads continued on the other sides as well, making a total of three hundred and sixty-six heads.[4] But the new data from the Proyecto 80-82, which included in-depth studies of the north and south faces, indicate that the monument had seven, not six, stepped sections, with a respective increase in the total number of heads adorning the monument.[5]

Around the Templo de Quetzalcoatl various burials have been found, arranged symmetrically along the north and south external sides. The discovery of two individual burials at the north and south sides of the building prompted archaeologists to make further explorations. In 1983-1984 another individual burial was discovered and subsequently a multiple burial containing the remains of

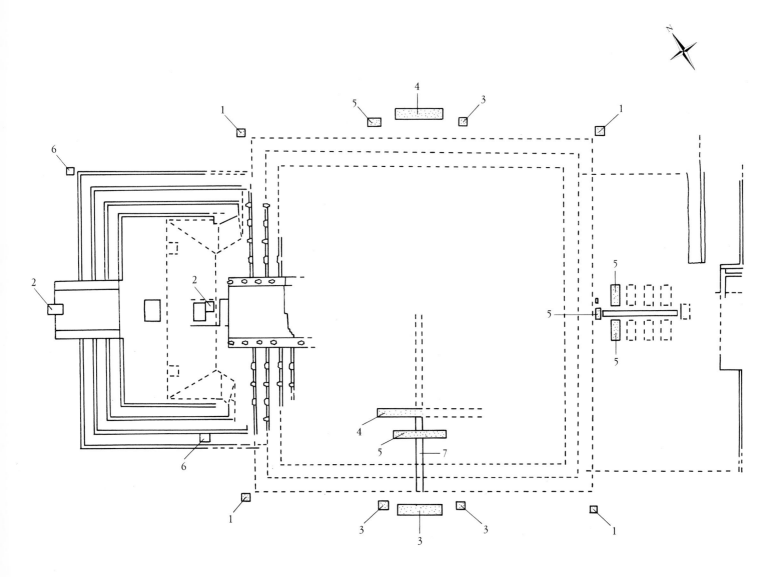

212

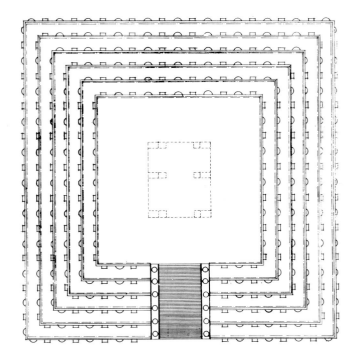

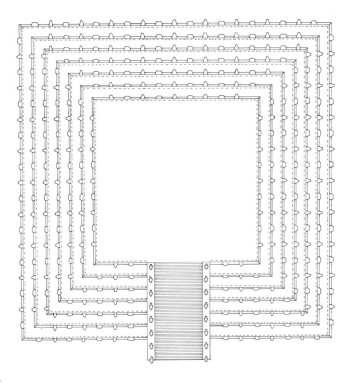

eighteen human sacrificial victims. This important find suggested the existence of further burials at the north and west side of the building. In 1985 a similar multiple burial was dug up, containing yet another eighteen richly adorned sacrificial victims.

This series of discoveries, which till then had no equivalent in the archaeology of Teotihuacán and shed new light on its history, prompted a separate project for the full exploration of the Templo de Quetzalcoatl and the land around it. The first study of the Proyecto Templo de Quetzalcoatl, undertaken in 1988, was financed by the United States National Science Foundation. The second, which is still under way (1989), is being financed by the U.S.-based National Geographic Society, under the direction of Rubén Cabrera Castro of the Instituto Nacional de Antropología e Historia in Mexico City, and of George Cowgill of Brandeis University, Massachusetts.

This project aims to solve a variety of problems. On the one hand, it will include an inquiry into the kind of government presiding in Teotihuacán, the function of religion and the basic values of its culture (until very recently it was thought that Teotihuacán was an eminently theocratic state, in view of the prevalence of religious features throughout the city). On the other hand, an investigation must be made into the role of military affairs within the state apparatus, of which very little is recorded in the city's iconography. In contrast, the murals, pottery and other archaeological relics portray a great many deities, priests and sacred scenes. The question is whether this society was as stable as it has been claimed, whether it experienced a long and continuous development or whether this was interrupted by conflicts and social crises. Such upheavals would have resulted in considerable alterations in the State's organization and structure.

The Proyecto Templo de Quetzalcoatl considered that one of the best places of the city to answer these questions was the Ciudadela, the most probable site of the aristocracy's homes and the seat of power itself. Given the construction of the place (with its high surrounding wall) and the new data that has emerged on the Templo de Quetzalcoatl (and on human sacrifice), it now seems legitimate to assume that it

111. Two possible reconstructions of the Templo de Quetzalcoatl. The one on the left proposes six stepped sections (from Marquina, 1951), and the one on the right seven, as suggested by the Proyecto Arqueológico Teotihuacán (from Cabrera and Sugiyama, 1980-82).

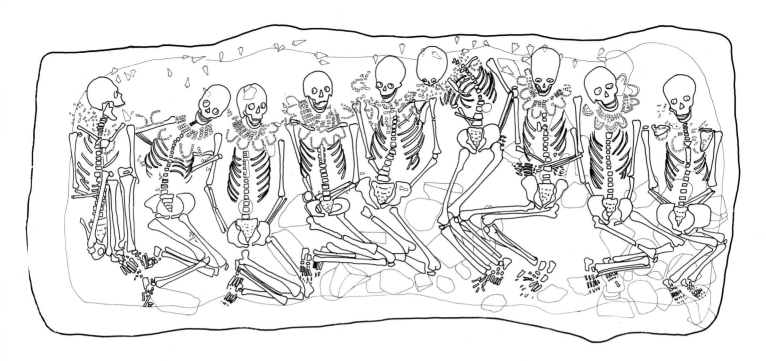

112. Multiple burial with nine human skeletons found on the east side of the Templo de Quetzalcoatl.

was indeed the political and administrative focus of the Teotihuacán government.

Once the voluminous data so far gathered from the Proyecto Teotihuacán 80-82 and the Proyecto Templo de Quetzalcoatl have been elaborated, questions of this kind should be cleared up. The most important finds from these excavations, especially considering their originality compared with earlier finds in the Teotihuacán area, are the human burials and their offerings. They are symmetrically arranged both inside and outside the temple, in ditches dug in the *tepetate* (a lava stone) and in tombs surrounded by stone walls. Some of the burials contain a single skeleton, others groups of four, eight, nine, eighteen or twenty-six skeletons, all aligned toward the central part of the building. The huddled position of the bodies, with their arms behind their backs and hands joined as if bound together, is clear evidence that they were sacrificial victims.

The burials also yielded a rich array of ornaments: necklaces of shells and green stones, earrings and *narigueras* (nose pendants), shell pendants carved in the form of human jawbones, and even real human jawbones. Other skeletons have been found, with pendants fashioned from animal jawbones (either dog or coyote). These types of ornaments were traditionally worn by warriors.

If we discount the burials discovered during the 1917-1922 project (the excavation records only speak of secondary burials found in the upper part of the building), the burials unearthed so far total ninety-six, and all have similar characteristics. But considering the symmetrical pattern of those found (see Figure 110 on page 212), it may well be that the number of individuals immolated and buried both within and outside the temple will reach around two hundred and twenty, dating from the time the construction was commenced to the time it was completed.

According to studies carried out on the skeletal remains, the victims were all male, aged between sixteen and forty-five. Some of the bodies must have been of people of high rank, as they show skull deformations, and several have mutilated teeth and dental incrustations of greenstone, turquoise, and bone. In some burials, slate disks or clasps have been found at the body's back, presumably part of the victim's clothing. Other items among the burial goods include many obsidian blade points arranged around the victim's skull.

Judging from the position and arrangement both within and outside the Templo

113. 114. Details of skeletons 6B and 5D found in the burials on the east side of the Templo de Quetzalcoatl. The arms linked behind their backs, and hands joined as if bound, suggest these are bodies of sacrificial victims.

de Quetzalcoatl in accordance with the four cardinal points, and from the number of individuals buried together (1, 4, 8, 9, 18 and 26), it would seem that the burials corresponded to astronomical and calendar calculations and hence to crop cycles. Their exact meaning however is still unclear.

This information is of vital importance for understanding the foundations of Teotihuacán civilization. What was the real role of the military? While it has usually been assumed that the city's government was eminently theocratic, the data gathered here suggests the opposite, at least for the earlier phases of Teotihuacán's development. The vast numbers of sacrificial victims seem to indicate a ruthless, despotic government. What is the meaning behind the extensive human sacrificial rites carried out in Teotihuacán? Were the victims citizens of Teotihuacán or outsiders? These and many other questions raised by the new finds have yet to be answered.

The Plaza 2 and the Cuadrángulo Norte

The Cuadrángulo Norte lies in the northwestern corner of a vast rectangular clearing, called Plaza 2, running the full length of the north side of the Gran Plataforma. From its proximity and the activities performed there, we can assume that the complex was functionally linked to the Ciudadela itself.

At first the Plaza 2 was thought to be an open area without buildings, given the scarcity of remains found on surface level. But excavations soon revealed more than anyone had remotely expected.

The external section of the Plaza 2, nearest the Avenue of the Dead, revealed a dense series of structural alterations and improvements to the dwellings, evidenced by the floors and walling next to the wall bordering the Plaza. Burials of children were also found here, their bones stored in clay vases. On the north side, excavations uncovered the remains of a vast set of steps constructed over a series of

215

cells built with *adobe* bricks, using the recurrent technique of a mixture of rubble, stone and earth to form an inner core.

Within the clearing itself, excavations were concentrated on the extreme northwestern end, where a special area designated as the Cuadrángulo Norte was marked out. Here were found the remains of two circular buildings, the plan of a small *temescal* (steam bath), the only one of its kind so far unearthed in Teotihuacán, a set of three rooms arranged in typical Teotihuacán fashion, and a workshop of high quality pottery with over thirty thousand molds and clay reproductions for use on ritual braziers. Close to the workshop, numerous work tools were found, together with a stock of unworked clay and two kilns for firing the pots, built in the open.

Much has been said regarding the manufacturing activity in Teotihuacán—the city must have housed a great many artisans specializing in a wide range of products. The confirmation was the discovery of this workshop specialized in the production of fine ware, linked to the Ciudadela, from where it is assumed that the city was controlled and administrated.

We can infer from the context that this workshop addressed the needs of those living in the Ciudadela, and (judging from the quantity of molds found) that many units of specialized artisans were involved in the production of fine pottery vessels. Such activity was a sign of the power wielded by the elite, but it was also a means of ideological control.

115. Serpent head with forked tongue. Stairway of the West Plaza Complex, Avenue of the Dead, earlier construction phase (see Plate 99).

Sculpture

Recent excavations have provided a liberal selection of sculpture pieces of varying kinds, many of them depicting feline forms or serpent heads; there are also numerous anthropomorphic figures, water deities and fertility gods.

Specimens of monumental sculpture carved from massive blocks of stone were normally part of the architecture, such as the huge frieze found in the West Plaza Complex of the Avenue of the Dead. This frieze is made up of several joined slabs and portrays the water deity Tlaloc. Regrettably, it is incomplete, but it is possible to reconstruct the missing sections. The figure of Tlaloc is wearing an imposing headdress (depicting birds, plants and serpent heads) crowned with an elaborate fan of feathers. The figure is wearing earrings and a *nariguera* or nose ornament. Among the various motifs near his hands, there are two streams of water.

In the same architectural complex another building has come to light, whose imposing stairway shows two distinct construction phases denoting two different epochs in Teotihuacán's development. In the earlier construction phase, contemporay with the final period of the Templo de Quetzalcoatl, the lower part of the stair *alfarda* was decorated with stone serpent heads. These have big forked tongues and both feline and human features, thus proving the acute religious crises that shook Teotihuacán in this epoch.

116. Jaguar head. Stairway of the West Plaza Complex, Avenue of the Dead, later construction phase (see Plate 98).

In the later construction phase, corresponding to the last presence of Teotihuacán in this place, the serpent heads were covered by a layer of infill and the upper part of the stair *alfarda* was decorated with jaguar heads.

In the complex of the West Plaza of the Avenue of the Dead, excavations yielded another specimen of exceptional artistic value. The sculpture in question is made from serpentine and portrays a female figure wearing a skirt, a *quezquemitl* or shawl-shaped blouse, and a headdress adorned with finely carved frets and interlaced patterns. The figure was found near a small altar in one of the rooms in the complex, which may mean that it represented a family deity, as has been noted elsewhere in Teotihuacán culture.

These examples of sculpture not directly related to architecture, such as the female figure just mentioned, are part of an ample range of specimens discovered in more recent excavations. They include images of jaguars, serpents and particularly anthropomorphic figures, as well as many masks carved from andesite, basalt or serpentine, which are characteristic of Teotihuacán style.

117. Teotihuacán mask in serpentine, a stone found in the state of Guerrero. Height 6½ inches.

Pottery

In this field too, vital new data has emerged: recently unearthed specimens, though generally of the same form and style, have provided some variations that enable us to understand the basic shapes and production development.

Some of the pottery vessels show the typical features of outside contemporary cultures. This tends to confirm the idea of the frequent contact with the metropolis, and hence its influence and prestige throughout Mesoamerica.

The new findings include the distinctive Teotihuacan tripod cylinder jars with slab-shaped legs. Some of them are fresco-painted with deities or vegetal designs like plants, flowers and fruit.There are also hemispherical bowls in coffe-colored ware picturing a deity (Tlaloc) alternating with other symbolic motifs; small animal-patterned Thin Orange pottery vases with pierced animal-shaped handles used as musical instruments; disks or seals in San Martín Orange ware, bearing the image of the water deity Tlaloc with other symbolic motifs; and lastly, a pottery pipe, the only example of this kind found in Teotihuacán among objects of daily usage.

One of the various pieces found in Teotihuacán in which we can detect outside

118. Pipe. Clay,
height 2 inches.

influence is a tripod vase with bored supports in the form of *almenas* (merlons), its body decorated with scrolls and scribbles typical of pottery from El Tajín, a culture that developed during the Classic Mesoamerican period along the coast of Veracruz.

Another small vase with anthropomorphic designs also indicates the influence of El Tajín: it bears the face of a bearded man, quite atypical to come from models outside the Mesoamerican culture.

Conclusions

This breakdown of the new finds resulting from the latest excavations in Teotihuacán is, of course, very brief. It reports the most important results of the Proyecto Arqueológico Teotihuacán 80-82 and those of the ongoing Proyecto Templo de Quetzalcoatl, without considering other important studies conducted by archaeologists in various points of Teotihuacán—studies which deal with specific themes, providing key insights into this culture.

Thanks to recent analyses, to the new methods and techniques adopted both in the archaeological digs and in the laboratory, we are reaching a more realistic understanding of the cultural development of Teotihuacán in all its many phases—thanks also to vast quantities of new data accumulated, some of which have yet to be analyzed, and some of which have already been published in detail.

The study of all this material has guided experts toward more specific areas of inquiry, such as the study of Teotihuacán architecture and urban development, and the various phases of construction and expansion. Unprecedented progress has been made in establishing Teotihuacán's chronology. There is new evidence of the existence of outside groups settled in various neighborhoods throughout the metropolis, and definitive proof of workshops specialized in the creation of pottery, sculpture and other products.

We now have further information on the mathematical knowledge of the

119. Molds and clay reproductions found in a workshop of high quality pottery, Cuadrángulo Norte of the Ciudadela.

Teotihuacán, their units of measurement, grasp of astronomy, means of calculating time and agricultural cycles. It is of particular interest to ascertain what knowledge the peasants had of farming and hydraulics. And lastly, recent evidence of frequent human sacrifice once more raises the major issue of the purpose and function of such rites, religiously and politically.

The results of all these in-depth studies will provide us with a greater knowledge of Teotihuacán culture, a culture that exerted a considerable influence on contemporary Mesoamerican societies and represented a model for the development of later cultures.

120. Disk or seal in San Martín Orange ware, bearing the image of Tlaloc with other symbolic motifs.

Notes to the Text

INTRODUCTION

1. *Anales de Cuauhtitlán*, 1975.
2. León-Portilla, 1976.

CHAPTER 1

1. MacNeish, 1967.
2. Niederberger, 1987.
3. Barba de Piña Chan, 1956. Piña Chan, 1958.
4. Cummings, 1933.
5. Serra Puche, 1979.

CHAPTER 2

1. López Luján, 1989. Matos Moctezuma, in press.
2. Sahagún, 1950-1982.
3. Mendieta, 1870.
4. Torquemada, 1977.
5. Paso y Troncoso, 1905-1906.
6. Sahagún, 1950-1982.
7. Bernal, 1979.
8. Gemelli Carreri, 1699-1700.
9. Clavigero, 1958.
10. Humboldt, 1814.
11. Calderón de la Barca, 1931.
12. Almaraz, 1865.
13. Charnay, 1887.
14. Bernal, 1979.
15. Chavero, 1884.
16. Chavero, 1884.
17. Mendoza, 1877.
18. Bancroft, 1883.
19. Holmes, 1885.
20. Nuttall, 1886.
21. García Cubas, 1906.
22. Peñafiel, 1900.
23. Batres, 1906.
24. Gamio, 1922.
25. Newell, 1902.
26. Hagar, 1910.
27. Barnett, 1912.
28. Boas, 1912.
29. Seler, 1912.
30. Seler, 1915.
31. Gamio, 1922.
32. Gamio, 1922.
33. Gamio, 1922.
34. Gamio, 1922.
35. Villa Aguilera, n.d.
36. Linné, 1934.
37. Noguera, 1935.
38. Vaillant, 1938.
39. Caso, 1942.
40. Armillas, 1944.
41. Millon, 1954.
42. Acosta, 1964.
43. Sejourné, 1959.
44. Bernal, 1963. Acosta, 1964.
45. Sanders, 1965.
46. Sanders, 1965, suggests that some villages were probably devoted to the intensive manufacture of weapons for war.
47. Millon, 1973.
48. Rattray, 1979.
49. McClung, 1978.
50. Spence, 1967.
51. Cowgill, 1968.
52. Cabrera, 1982.

CHAPTER 3

1. The *chinampas* cultivation system was practiced on swampy terrain. Ditches were dug in which the water flowed, and erosion was prevented by lining the banks with posts, and trees whose roots anchored the soil. The highly-fertile earth from the ditches was used to consolidate the new plot itself.
2. Caso, 1942.
3. Millon, 1957.
4. Sanders, 1965.
5. Gamio, 1922.
6. Millon, 1973.
7. Millon, 1973.

CHAPTER 4

1. Matos Moctezuma, 1974-76. In Part Two of *Proyecto Tula*, I suggested that the Tula area was under Teotihuacán control, owing to the discovery of calcareous stones there.

2. Millon, 1973.
3. Spence, 1987.
4. Cowgill, 1984.
5. McClung, 1987.
6. Millon, 1981.
7. Rattray, 1987.

CHAPTER 5

1. Sejourné, 1959.
2. Saenz, 1962.
3. Armillas, 1951.
4. Piña Chan, 1960.

APPENDIX

1. Gamio, 1922.
2. Cabrera Castro, 1982.
3. Cabrera Castro, Rodriguez, and Morelos, 1982.
4. Marquina, 1951.
5. Cabrera Castro, and Sugiyama, 1982.

Bibliography

ABBREVIATIONS: INAH, Instituto Nacional de Antropología e Historia
UNAM, Universidad Nacional Autónoma de México

ACOSTA, JORGE R.
1964 *El Palacio del Quetzalpapalotl*. Memorias no. 10. Mexico City: INAH.

1978 *Teotihuacán, Official Guide*. Mexico City: INAH.

ALMARAZ, RAMÓN
1865 Apuntes sobre las Pirámides de San Juan Teotihuacán. In *Memoria de los Trabajos Efectuados por la Comisión Científica de Pachuca en el Ãno 1864*, 349–358. Mexico City.

ANALES DE CUAUHTITLÁN
1975 Translated from the Náhuatl by Primo F. Velázquez. Mexico City: UNAM, Instituto de Investigaciones Historicas.

ARMILLAS, PEDRO
1944 Exploraciones Recientes en Teotihuacán, México. *Cuadernos Americanos* (Mexico City) vol. 16, no. 4: 121–136.

1951 Tecnología, Formaciones Socioecónomicas y Religión en Mesoamérica. In *Actas del Congreso Internacional de Americanistas*.

BANCROFT, H.
1883 *Native Races*, vol. 1. San Francisco.

BARBA DE PIÑA CHAN, BEATRÍZ
1956 *Tlapacoya: un Sitio Pre-Clásico de Transición*. Acta Antropológica, época 2. Mexico City: INAH.

BARNETT, MADAME
1912 Quelques Observations sur les Petites Têtes de Teotihuacán. In *Actas del 18 Congreso Internacional de Americanistas, London*.

BATRES, LEOPOLDO
1906 Teotihuacán, Memoria que presenta Leopoldo Batres. In *Actas del 15 Congreso Internacional de Americanistas, Quebec*. Mexico City: Imprenta de Fidencio Soria.

BERNAL, IGNACIO
1963   *Teotihuacán: Descubrimientos, Reconstrucciones*. Mexico City: INAH.

1979   *Historia de la Arqueología en México*. Mexico City: Editorial Porrúa.

BOAS, FRANZ
1912   Archaeological Investigations in the Valley of Mexico by International School. In *Actas del 18 Congreso Internacional de Americanistas, London*.

BRAMBILA, ROSA
1986   *Sala de Teotihuacán. Museo Nacional de Antropología*. Mexico City: García Valadés Editores.

CABRERA CASTRO, RUBÉN (ed.)
1982   *Memoria del Proyecto Arqueológico Teotihuacán*. Colección Científica no. 132. Mexico City: INAH.

CABRERA CASTRO, RUBÉN, AND S. SUGIYAMA
1982   La Exploracion y Restauracion del Templo Viejo de Quetzalcoatl. In *Memoria del Proyecto Arqueologico Teotihuacán*. Colección Científica no. 132. Mexico City: INAH.

CABRERA CASTRO, RUBÉN, IGNACIO RODRIGUEZ, AND NOEL MORELOS (eds.)
1982   *Teotihuacán 80–82. Primeros Resultados*. Mexico City: INAH.

CALDERÓN DE LA BARCA, FANNY
1931   *Life in Mexico During a Residence of Two Years in That Country*. New York: Dutton.

CASO, ALFONSO
1942   El Paraíso Terrenal en Teotihuacán. *Cuadernos Americanos* (Mexico City) vol. 1, no. 6: 127–36.

CHARNAY, DÉSIRÉ
1887   Les Anciennes Villes du Nouveau Monde (first edition 1885. Paris: Hachette).
        Translated as *The Ancient Cities of the New World*. New York: Harper and Brothers.

CHAVERO, ALFREDO
1884   *México a Través de los Siglos*. Mexico City: Ballesco.

CLAVIGERO, PADRE FRANCESCO SAVERIO
1958   *Storia Antica del Messico cavata da' migliori Spagnoli e da' Manoscritti e dalle Pitture Antiche degli Indiani* (first edition 1780–81. Cesena, Italy: Biasini Editore). Translated as *Historia Antigua de México*. Mexico City: Editorial Porrúa.

COE, MICHAEL D.
1964   *Mexico. Ancient Peoples and Places*. New York: Praeger.

COVARRUBIAS, MIGUEL
1957   *Indian Art of Mexico and Central America*. New York: A. Knopf.

COWGILL, GEORGE
1968   Computer Analysis of Archaeological Data from Teotihuacán, Mexico. In *New Perspectives in Archaeology*, edited by Sally and Lewis R. Binford. New York: Aldine.

COWGILL, GEORGE, JEFFREY ALTSCHUL, AND REBECCA SLOAD
1984   Spatial Analysis of Teotihuacán: A Mesoamerican Metropolis. In *Intrasite Spatial Analysis in Archaeology*, edited by Harold Hietala. Cambridge: Cambridge University Press.

CUMMINGS, BYRON
1933   *Cuicuilco and the Archaic Culture of Mexico*. Social Science Bulletin no. 4. Tucson: University of Arizona.

GAMIO, MANUEL
1922   *La Población del Valle de Teotihuacán*, 3 vols. Mexico City: Secretaría de Agricultura y Fomento, Departamento de Arqueología y Etnografía (1979 facsimile edition. Mexico City: Instituto Nacional Indigenista).

GARCÍA CUBAS, ANTONIO
1906   Mis Últimas Exploraciones Arqueológicas. In *Memorias de la Sociedad Científica Antonio Alzate*, vol. 24. Mexico City.

GEMELLI CARRERI, GIOVANNI FRANCESCO
1699–1700 *Giro del Mondo*, 6 vols. Naples.

HAGAR, STANSBURY
1910   The Celestial Plan of Teotihuacán. In *Actas del Congreso Internacional de Americanistas, Mexico City*.

HOLMES, WILLIAM
1885   The Monoliths of San Juan Teotihuacán. *The American Journal of Archaeology* (Baltimore) vol. 1, no. 4.

HUMBOLDT, ALEXANDER VON
1814   *Vue des Cordillères, et Monuments des Peuples Indigènes de l'Amérique* (first edition 1810, 2 vols. Paris: F. Schoell). Translated as *Researches Concerning the Institutions and Monuments of the Ancient Inhabitants of America*. London.

LEÓN-PORTILLA, MIGUEL
1976   *Los Antiguos Mexicanos a Través de sus Crónicas y Cantares*. Mexico City: Fondo de Cultura Económica.

LINNÉ, SIGVALD
1934   *Archaeological Researches at Teotihuacán, Mexico*. Publication no. 1, Ethnographical Museum of Sweden. Stockholm: Victor Pettersons.

LÓPEZ LUJÁN, LEONARDO
1989   *La Recuperación Mexica del Pasado Teotihuacano*. Mexico City: INAH.

MacNEISH, RICHARD
1967   A Summary of the Subsistence. In *Prehistory of the Tehuacán Valley*. Vol. 1 *Environment and Subsistence*, edited by D.S. Byers, 290–309. Austin: University of Texas Press.

MARQUINA, IGNACIO
1951   *Arquitectura Prehispánica*. Mexico City: INAH.

MATOS MOCTEZUMA, EDUARDO (ed.)
1974–76 *Proyecto Tula. Primera y Segunda Parte*. Colección Científica nos. 15, 33. Mexico City: INAH.

1988   *Cacaxtla*. Photos by Rafael Donis. Mexico City: Citicorp.

in press Teotihuacán y Tenochtitlan. In *Cinco Ensayos acerca de los Mexicas*. Mexico City: García Valadés Editores.

McCLUNG DE TAPIA, EMILY
1978   Aspectos Ecológicos del Desarrollo y la Decadencia de Teotihuacán. In *Anales de Antropología*, no. 15. Mexico City: UNAM.

1987   Patrones de Subsistencia Urbana en Teotihuacán. In *Teotihuacán*. Mexico City: UNAM.

MENDIETA, FRAY JERÓNIMO DE
1870   *Historia Eclesiástica Indiana*. Mexico City.

MENDOZA, GUMERSINDO
1877   Article in *Anales del Museo Nacional*. Mexico City.

MILLON, RENÉ
1954   Irrigation at Teotihuacán. *American Antiquity* (Salt Lake City) vol. 20: 177–180.

1957   Irrigation System in the Valley of Teotihuacán. *American Antiquity* (Salt Lake City) vol. 23.

1973   *Urbanization at Teotihuacán*, vol. 1, parts 1–2, edited by René Millon, Bruce Drewitt, and George Cowgill. Austin: University of Texas Press.

1981   Teotihuacán: City, State, and Civilization. *In Handbook of Middle American Indians*. Austin: University of Texas Press.

NEWELL, WARDLE
1902   Certain Clay Figures of Teotihuacán. In *Actas del 13 Congreso Internacional de Americanistas, New York*.

NIEDERBERGER, CHRISTINE
1987   *Paléopaysages et Archéologie Pré-Urbaine du Bassin du Mexico*, 2 vols. Mexico City: Centro de Estudios de México y Centroamérica.

NOGUERA, EDUARDO
1935   Antecedentes y Relaciones de la Cultura Teotihuacana. *El México Antiguo* (Mexico City) vol. 3, nos. 5–8: 3–90, 93–95.

NUTTALL, ZELIA
1886   Terracotta Heads of San Juan Teotihuacán. *The American Journal of Archaeology* (Baltimore) vol. 2.

PASO Y TRONCOSO, FRANCISCO DEL
1905–1906   *Papeles de la Nueva España*. Madrid.

PEÑAFIEL, ANTONIO
1900   *Teotihuacán*. Mexico City: Secretaría de Fomento.

PIÑA CHAN, ROMÁN
1958   *Tlatilco*. Serie Investigaciones, nos. 1–2. Mexico City: INAH.

1960   *Mesoamérica*. Memoria no. 6. Mexico City: INAH.

1972   *Historia, Arqueología y Arte Prehispánico*. Mexico City.

RATTRAY, EVELYN
1979   La Cerámica de Teotihuacán: Relaciones Externas y Cronología. In *Anales de Antropología*, no. 15. Mexico City: UNAM.

1987   Los Barrios Foráneos de Teotihuacán. In *Teotihuacán*. Mexico City: UNAM.

SÁENZ, CÉSAR A.
1962   *Quetzalcoatl*. Mexico City: INAH.

SAHAGÚN, FRAY BERNARDINO DE
1950–1982   *Codex Florentinus or Mediceo Palatino 218–220* (original manuscript 1565–77, at Biblioteca Medicea Laurenziana, Florence). Translated from the Náhuatl by Arthur J. O. Anderson and Charles E. Dibble as *Florentine Codex, General History of the Things of New Spain*, 13 vols. Santa Fe: The School of American Research and the University of Utah.

SANDERS, WILLIAM
1965   *The Cultural Ecology of the Teotihuacán Valley: a Preliminary Report of the Results of the Teotihuacán Valley Project.* University Park: The Pennsylvania State University Press.

SEJOURNÉ, LAURETTE
1959   *Un Palacio en la Ciudad de los Dioses: Exploraciones en Teotihuacán 1955–58.* Mexico City: INAH.

SELER, EDUARD
1912   Similarity of Design of Some Teotihuacán Frescoes and Certain Mexican Pottery Objects. In *Actas del 18 Congreso Internacional de Americanistas, London.*

1915   *Die Teotihuacán Kultur des Jochlandes von Mexico*, vol. 5. In *Gesammelte Abhandlungen zur Amerikanischen Sprach-und Altertumskunde*, 5 vols. and index, 1902–1923. Berlin.

SERRA PUCHE, MARICARMEN, AND SERGIURA YAMAMOTO
1979   Terremote-Tlaltenco, D.F. In *Anales de Antropología*, no. 21. Mexico City: UNAM.

SIGÜENZA Y GÓNGORA, CARLOS DE
1928   *Obras con una Biografía escrita por Francisco Perez Salazar.* Mexico City: Sociedad de Bibliófilas Mexicanos.

SPENCE, MICHAEL
1967   The Obsidian Industry of Teotihuacán. *American Antiquity* vol. 32, no. 4.

1987   The Scale and Structure of Obsidian Production in Teotihuacán. In *Teotihuacán.* Mexico City: UNAM.

TORQUEMADA, FRAY JUAN DE
1977   *Monarquía Indiana* (first edition 1723). Mexico City: UNAM.

VAILLANT, GEORGE
1938   A Correlation of Archaeological and Historical Sequences in the Valley of Mexico. *American Anthropologist* (New York) vol. 40: 535–73.

VILLA AGUILERA, MANUEL
n.d.   La Obra de Manuel Gamio en la Historia de la Investigación Social en México. Unpublished manuscript.

WILLEY, GORDON
1966   *North and Middle America*, vol. 1 of *An Introduction to American Archaeology.* Engelwood Cliffs, New Jersey: Prentice Hall.

List of Plates

18. The altar at the center of the Ciudadela. Behind this, the building with four "talud-tablero" levels built over the Templo de Quetzalcoatl, the tip of which is just visible.

19. Detail of the altar at the center of the Ciudadela. In the background, the north side of the raised Gran Plataforma enclosing the Ciudadela.

20. The altar at the center of the Ciudadela clearing, seen from the west.

21. The raised Gran Plataforma enclosing the Ciudadela, seen from inside. Note the three double orders of steps and three pyramid bases.

22. Polychrome mural on a building within the Ciudadela.

23. Right, the Templo de Quetzalcoatl. 208 feet square. Miccaotli Phase, A.D. 150-250. Left, building with four "talud-tablero" levels which in the successive Tlamimilolpa Phase covered the temple completely.

24. Tripod vase with priest scattering seeds on the ground. Terracotta with engraved decoration, height 4^1/$_2$ inches. Museo Nacional de Antropología, Mexico City.

25. Fragment of tripod vase with talking figure. Terracotta with relief and engraved decoration, height 7 inches. Museo Nacional de Antropología, Mexico City.

26. Tripod vase with priests. Terracotta with relief polychrome decoration, height 6 inches. Museo Nacional de Antropología, Mexico City.

27. 28. Two priests in procession scattering seeds on the ground. Details from the Tepantitla murals, Teotihuacán.

29. Detail of lower panel of the Tlalocan Mural at Tepantitla, Teotihuacán. Replica, Museo Nacional de Antropología, Mexico City. The panel is thought to represent the paradise of the god Tlaloc or, more probably, scenes from earthly life (see Figures 85 and 86 on page 178).

30. Seated figure with elaborate headdress. Terracotta. Museo Nacional de Antropología, Mexico City.

31. Old man. Carved and polished terracotta, height 6 inches. Museo Nacional de Antropología, Mexico City.

32. Reclining figure. Terracotta, height 4^1/$_2$ inches. Museo Nacional de Antropología, Mexico City.

33. Anthropomorphic sculpture.

34. Effigy vessel. Dark terracotta, height 8 inches. Museo Nacional de Antropología, Mexico City.

35. Effigy vessel. Ceramic, height 7 inches Museo Nacional de Antropología, Mexico City.

36. Ceramic vase.

37. "Candelero" or incense burner. Terracotta, height 2^1/$_2$ inches. Museo Nacional de Antropología, Mexico City.

38. "Anaranjado Delgado" or Thin Orange pottery vessel, with three tiny spherical supports called "soportes-botón."

39. Common bowl. Terracotta, height 8 inches. Museo Nacional de Antropología, Mexico City.

40. Figurine with movable limbs, perhaps used as a toy. Terracotta, height 12 inches. Museo Nacional de Antropología, Mexico City.

41. The stone stairway of the Templo de Quetzalcoatl in the Ciudadela. Miccaotli Phase, A.D. 150-250.

42. A set of "talud" and "tablero" slabs in the Templo de Quetzalcoatl. "Tablero" slabs are decorated alternately with serpent heads and heads of a deity seen frontally, with the body of the serpent and various shells at intervals. "Talud" slab bears the head and the body of the serpent seen in profile.

43. A plumed serpent head on a "tablero" in the Templo de Quetzalcoatl. Everything was painted with mineral colors, faint traces of which still remain.

44. 45. Heads of deities in the Templo de Quetzalcoatl.

46. Northern "alfarda" of the stairway up the Templo de Quetzalcoatl, showing serpent heads one above the other.

47. Northern "tablero" of the Templo de Quetzalcoatl, with a serpent head and heads of a deity.

48. Serpent head at the entrance to the Palacio del

Quetzalpapalotl or "Quetzal-Butterfly," Xolalpan Phase, A.D. 450-650.

49. Pillar with bas-relief of bird seen in profile. Inner courtyard of the Palacio del Quetzalpapalotl.

50. Inner courtyard of the Palacio del Quetzalpapalotl. At left, two pillars from the west side with bas-reliefs of birds seen frontally. Note the "almenas" or merlons with the symbol of the year above the polychrome cornice.

51. Bird head seen frontally on a west pillar of the inner courtyard of the Palacio del Quetzalpapalotl.

52. Bird head seen in profile on a pillar of the inner courtyard of the Palacio del Quetzalpapalotl.

53. A plumed snail. Bas-relief on stone with traces of polychrome paint. Detail from the outer facade of the Palacio de los Caracoles Emplumados (Tlamimilolpa Phase, A.D. 250-450), beneath the Palacio del Quetzalpapalotl.

54. Stylized snails. Mural on the plinth of the inner courtyard portico of the Palacio del Quetzalpapalotl.

55. Detail from a mural in the Patio Blanco at Atetelco.

56. 57. Two pumas. Details from murals in the Patio Blanco at Atetelco, Teotihuacán. Xolalpan Phase, A.D. 450-650.

58. 59. Details of two birds in flight spouting water from their beaks. Murals on the outer base of the Palacio de los Caracoles Emplumados. Tlamimilolpa Phase, A.D. 250-450.

60. Man in water collecting snails in a net, from Tetitla murals, Teotihuacán. Xolalpan Phase, A.D. 450-650.

61. Diagrammatic representation of buildings. Tetitla murals.

62. Old man with beard. Tetitla murals.

63. Richly dressed deity scattering gifts on the ground. From his open hands flow jets of water containing small snails. Tetitla murals, Teotihuacán.

64. Detail of deity scattering gifts on the ground. Tetitla murals.

65. Orange-colored puma with headdress. Tetitla murals, Teotihuacán.

66. Head of dog or coyote. Tetitla murals.

67. Bird seen frontally, with wings outstretched. Tetitla murals.

68. Bird seen in profile. Tetitla murals.

69. Jaguar blowing a shell. Mural in the Patio de los Jaguares (Xolalpan Phase, A.D. 450-650), behind the Palacio del Quetzalpapalotl.

70. Head of the god Tlaloc at the center of a shell. Detail of mural reproduced above.

71. Large skull surrounded by rays, found in front of the Sun Pyramid. Stone with traces of red paint. Museo Nacional de Antropología, Mexico City. The sculpture symbolizes the sun disappearing in the west to take the light to the world of the dead.

72. Stylized jaguar head. Stone, height $31^1/2$ inches. Museo Nacional de Antropología, Mexico City.

73. Skull, perhaps related to the cult of the dead, found near the Sun Pyramid. Stone, height 29 inches. Museo Nacional de Antropología, Mexico City.

74. Mask. Stone, height 7 inches. Museo Nacional de Antropología, Mexico City.

75. Mask. Stone encrusted with turquoise, red shell, mother-of-pearl and obsidian. Height without necklace $9^1/2$ inches. Museo Nacional de Antropología, Mexico City.

76. Chalchiutlicue, the water goddess, found near the Moon Pyramid. Stone, height 10 feet. Museo Nacional de Antropología, Mexico City.

77. Composite stela used for ball game. Found at La Ventilla, a site southwest of Teotihuacán. Stone, height $6^1/2$ feet. Museo Nacional de Antropología, Mexico City.

78. Mask. Semiprecious polished stone with inlaid obsidian eyes. Height 8 inches. Museo del Templo Mayor, Mexico City.

79. Detail of a vessel in the form of an imaginary bird. Terracotta with snail and red-shell decorations. Height 10 inches. Museo Nacional de Antropología, Mexico City.

80. 81. 82. 83. Huehueteotl, the old fire god, a deity originating in Cuicuilco, represented with a brazier on his head. Museo Nacional de Antropología, Mexico City.

84. Brazier. Polychrome terracotta, lid with molded decoration, height 22¹/₂ inches. Museo Nacional de Antropología, Mexico City. Braziers of this shape, exclusive to Teotihuacán, were used for burning "copal," a perfumed resin.

85. Brazier lid. Polychrome terracotta with molded decoration, height 10 inches. Museo Nacional de Antropología, Mexico City.

86. Sculpture with unidentified motif. Stone, height 42 inches. Museo Nacional de Antropología, Mexico City.

87. "Almena" or merlon, with the symbol of the year. Stone, height 34¹/₂ inches. Museo Nacional de Antropología, Mexico City. Similar to those decorating the cornice of the inner courtyard of the Palacio del Quetzalpapalotl.

88. "Almena" with the head of the god Tlaloc. Terracotta, height 19¹/₂ inches. Museo Nacional de Antropología, Mexico City. Probably originally mounted on a building's roof.

89. "Almena" with the head of the god Tlaloc. Height 29 inches. Museo Nacional de Antropología, Mexico City.

90. "Almena" in the form of a bird spouting water from its beak. Terracotta, height 18¹/₂ inches. Museo Nacional de Antropología, Mexico City.

91. Tripod vase. Dark terracotta with engraved and modeled decoration, height 6 inches. Museo Nacional de Antropología, Mexico City.

92. Vase with effigies of the god Tlaloc. Terracotta, height 7 inches. Museo Nacional de Antropología, Mexico City.

93. Zoomorphic "Anaranjado Delgado" pottery vessel, height 4 inches. Museo Nacional de Antropología, Mexico City.

94. The west stairway in the central courtyard of the West Plaza Complex of the Avenue of the Dead as it stands today: the photograph shows only the later construction phase, with one surviving jaguar head along the "alfarda" or sloping ramp.

95. The same stairway during the excavation work conducted by the Proyecto Arqueológico Teotihuacán 1980-82: the underlying earlier construction phase is also visible, showing two serpent heads with forked

tongues—in better repair than those from the later phase because they were protected under a layer of infill.

96. Central courtyard of the West Plaza Complex. The west stairway, with the jaguar head, is at the left. In the background, the Sun Pyramid.

97. West stairway of the central courtyard of the West Plaza Complex of the Avenue of the Dead.

98. Large jaguar stone head. West stairway of the central courtyard of the West Plaza Complex, seen in the later construction phase (see Plate 94).

99. Serpent head with forked tongue. Large monolithic sculpture with traces of polychrome paint. It shows the typical traits of the plumed serpent, together with feline and anthropomorphic features. West stairway of the West Plaza Complex, earlier construction phase (see Plate 95).

100. Representation of Tlaloc. Fragment of a large carved frieze made up of several joined stone slabs. It was found in the West Plaza Complex of the Avenue of the Dead. Museo Arqueológico de Teotihuacán.

101. Tripod vase with openwork supports in the form of "almenas." The scrolls and scribbles decoration is typical of El Tajín ware.

102. Female figure with "quezquemitl" or shawl-shaped blouse. Engraved polished serpentine. Found in the West Plaza Complex of the Avenue of the Dead.

103. Central courtyard of the West Plaza Complex of the Avenue of the Dead.

104. Northwest Complex of the San Juan river. In background at right, the Ciudadela. This recently excavated residential complex is situated at the corner where the river crosses the west side of the Avenue of the Dead.

105. 106. Northwest Complex of the San Juan river.

107. Northwest Complex of the San Juan river.

108. Structure with remains of decorated plaster. Northwest Complex of the San Juan river.

109. Tripod cylinder jar with slab-shaped supports. Fresco-painted decoration with flowers and fruit.

List of Illustrations in Text

probably the lid of a jar, with engraved scorpion decoration (from Gamio, 1922, Fig. 43).

21. Fragment of mural with plant and flower motifs. Height 13½ inches. Museo Nacional de Antropología, Mexico City.

22. In Teotihuacán timber was used for building walls, pillars and roofing (from Acosta, 1964, Fig. 101).

23. Map of Teotihuacán. Inset shows ceremonial precinct and residential sections. 1) Avenue of the Dead. 2) Ciudadela. 3) Templo de Quetzalcoatl. 4) Viking Group. 5) Palacio in front of the Sun Pyramid. 6) Sun Pyramid. 7) Palacio del Sol. 8) Jaguar Mural. 9) Xolalpan. 10) Merchants' Quarter. 11) Tlamimilolpa. 12) Tepantitla. 13) Modern roadway. 14) Moon Pyramid. 15) Templo de la Agricultura. 16) Templo de los Animales Mitológicos. 17) Palacio del Quetzalpapalotl (Quetzal-Butterfly) and underlying Palacio de los Caracoles Emplumados. 18) Patio de los Jaguares. 19) West Plaza Complex of the Avenue of the Dead. 20) Superimposed Buildings. 21) Northwest Complex of the San Juan river. 22) Yayahuala. 23) Zacuala. 24) Atetelco. 25) Tetitla. 26) San Juan river. 27) East-West Avenue. 28) Market.

24. Island with spring irrigating *chinampas*. Detail from the Tlalocan Mural in Tepantitla, Teotihuacán. Lower panel, bottom right corner.

25. Map of Teotihuacán drawn by René Millon (from Millon, 1973).

26. Urban expansion during the Tzacualli Phase.

27. Elevation and plan of the Sun Pyramid.

28. Reconstruction of the Moon Pyramid (from Acosta, 1978).

29. Elevation and plan of the Moon Pyramid.

30. Urban expansion during the Miccaotli Phase.

31. Reconstruction of the Templo de Quetzalcoatl in the Ciudadela, drawn by Ignacio Marquina (from Marquina, 1951).

32. Plan of the Ciudadela.

33. Plan of the Templo de Quetzalcoatl.

34. Urban expansion during the Tlamimilolpa Phase.

35. Palacio de los Caracoles Emplumados, with details of the murals of birds in flight (see Plates 58, 59).

36. Urban expansion during the Xolalpan Phase.

37. Plan of Tetitla, a residential section of Teotihuacán.

38. Entrance to the Palacio del Quetzalpapalotl with large serpent head at one side of stairway (see Plate 48) (from Acosta, 1964).

39. Patio de los Jaguares behind the Palacio del Quetzalpapalotl. In the background, the Moon Pyramid.

40. 41. Plan and reconstruction of Zacuala, a residential section of Teotihuacán.

42. 43. Plan of the Patio Central and reconstruction of the Patio Blanco (from Coe, 1964), both at Atetelco, a residential section of Teotihuacán.

44. Perspective plan of Xolalpan, a residential section of Teotihuacán (from Willey, 1966).

45. Plan of a building at Tepantitla, a residential section of Teotihuacán.

46. Urban expansion during the Metepec Phase.

47. Figure dressed as a jaguar, surrounded by glyphs. Detail from the murals at Cacaxtla, a site in the state of Tlaxcala.

48. Probable routes of communication and influence of Teotihuacán through Mesoamerica. Modern states are indicated.

49. Reconstructed plan of the main Cholula pyramid, state of Puebla.

50. Local variant of the Teotihuacán *talud-tablero* system used in the Cholula pyramid.

51. Three local variants of the Teotihuacán *talud-tablero* system used in the El Tajín pyramids, state of Veracruz.

52. Zapotec ceramic figure from the state of Oaxaca.

53. Zapotec ceramic urn, Monte Albán, Oaxaca (from Willey, 1966).

54. Pyramidal base with local variant of the

Teotihuacán *talud-tablero* system, Kaminaljuyú, Guatemala.

55. Priest. Murals from the Casa Barrios at the Teopancalco site, south of Teotihuacán (from Gamio, 1922, Plate 35).

56. Eagle warrior with darts and thrower.

57. Jaguar warrior. Zacuala murals, Teotihuacán.

58. Terracotta figurines showing the clothing of the Teotihuacán aristocracy. Many show intentional skull deformation. The last two on right are high-ranking women. Museo Nacional de Antropología, Mexico City.

59. Commoners. Tlalocan Mural in Tepantitla, Teotihuacán. Detail of lower panel.

60. Section of the inner core of a base. 1) Infill of *tezontle*, a volcanic rock, and *tepetate*, a rather insubstantial tufa, set in mud. 2) Fine plaster coat. 3) Mortar. 4) *Tepetate*. 5) Mortar. 6) Clay. 7) Mortar. 8) *Tepetate*. 9) River pebbles set in mud. 10) Adobe bricks. Below, the typical adobe or unbaked brick measuring approximately 21½ by 12 by 5 inches (from Gamio, 1922, Plate 16).

61. Small terracotta head. Museo Nacional de Antropología, Mexico City.

62. Female figurine with headdress, *quezquemitl* or shawl-like blouse, and skirt. Polychrome terracotta. Museo Nacional de Antropología, Mexico City.

63. Male figurine. Semiprecious stone. Museo Nacional de Antropología, Mexico City.

64. Male figurine with headdress, loincloth and sandals. Polychrome terracotta. Museo Nacional de Antropología, Mexico City.

65. Tools from Teotihuacán for 1) whittling and sawing; 2) sewing and spinning; 3) digging; 4) cutting; 5) beating; 6) grinding; 7) smoothing and polishing; 8) scraping; 9) piercing; 10) measuring (from Rosa Brambila, 1986).

66. Bone needles. Museo Nacional de Antropología, Mexico City.

67. Squash-shaped olla (from Gamio, 1922, Fig. 45).

68. Dog or coyote. Terracotta. Museo Nacional de Antropología, Mexico City.

69. Obsidian items. Museo Nacional de Antropología, Mexico City.

70. Plan of Tlamimilolpa, a residential section of Teotihuacán (from Willey, 1966).

71. Warrior with circular shield and three darts. Casa Barrios murals (from Gamio, 1922, Plate 77).

72. Representations of two temples. Bottom, a terracotta fragment. Top, detail from a mural in Tetitla, Teotihuacán (see Fig. 89 on page 179) (drawings by Covarrubias).

73. Tlaloc tripod vase, engraved terracotta, height 4 ½ inches. Museo Nacional de Antropología, Mexico City.

74. Tlaloc olla. Terracotta, height 6 inches. Museo Nacional de Antropología, Mexico City.

75. Small heads representing Xipe Totec, god of spring. Terracotta, height 1 inch. Museo Nacional de Antropología, Mexico City.

76. 77. Two images of Tlaloc in serpent form. Top, one of the stone heads that decorate the *tablero* blocks in the Templo de Quetzalcoatl. Bottom, stylized head of the god with forked tongue, stone bas-relief, 41 inches high, found in the Superimposed Buildings. Museo Nacional de Antropología, Mexico City (drawing at bottom by Miguel Covarrubias).

78. The god Huehueteotl. Stone, height 14 inches. Museo Nacional de Antropología, Mexico City.

79. Offering from a burial in Teotihuacán. Engraved pottery bowl, height 4 inches. Museo Nacional de Antropología, Mexico City.

80. 81. Two representations of the jaguar, symbol of Tlaloc. Top, stone vessel, British Museum, London. Bottom, stone mask (drawings by Covarrubias).

82. Construction phases of a *talud-tablero*. a) Infill of volcanic rock. b) Mortar and plaster. c) Pebbles set in mud. d) Andesite slab to hold up the *tablero*. e) Cornice of the *tablero*.

83. Anthropomorphic figure (top) and deity (bottom) with large headdress resembling head of owl. Terracotta figurines.

84. *Almenas* or merlons which crowned the roof of buildings.

85. Water deity with two assistants, upper panel of the Tlalocan Mural at Tepantitla, Teotihuacán. Replica, Museo Nacional de Antropología, Mexico City.

86. Scenes from earthly life, lower panel of the Tlalocan Mural at Tepantitla, Teotihuacán. Replica, Museo Nacional de Antropología, Mexico City (see Plate 29).

87. Detail of the mural in the Templo de los Animales Mitológicos, on the west side of the Avenue of the Dead. Replica, Museo Nacional de Antropología, Mexico City.

88. Fragment of column adorned with relief rings. Stone with remains of red paint, diameter 15 inches. Museo Nacional de Antropología, Mexico City.

89. Figure dressed as a jaguar heading toward a temple. Murals at Tetitla, Teotihuacán.

90. Detail of murals in the Templo de la Agricultura, on the west side of the Avenue of the Dead. Replica, Museo Nacional de Antropología, Mexico City.

91. Mask with earrings and *nariguera* or nose-pendant in the form of stylized butterfly. Polychrome terracotta.

92. Stone mask (from Willey, 1966).

93. Typical Teotihuacán mask. Circa A.D. 500. Semiprecious stone, height 6 inches. Museo Nacional de Antropología, Mexico City.

94. Olla with three handles. Terracotta, height 7 inches. Museo Nacional de Antropología, Mexico City. One or both the upper handles served for holding the receptacle, the lower one for pouring.

95. Tripod vase with slab-shaped legs. Terracotta with traces of fresco decoration, height 6 inches. Museo Nacional de Antropología, Mexico City. As in Figure 96, the cylinder base is encircled with rattles made from hollow spheres with a slit, each containing a small terracotta ball.

96. Fragment of a tripod vase depicting a figure beneath a cacao plant; a quetzal bird is perched in a branch overhead. Terracotta, height 4 inches.

97. Upper part of brazier lid. Polychrome ceramic with molded decorations.

98. *Florero* jar. Dark terracotta, height 4 inches. Museo Nacional de Antropología, Mexico City.

99. Cylindrical tripod vessel with lid. Engraved terracotta, height 11 inches.

100. Female figurine. Polychrome terracotta. Museo Nacional de Antropología, Mexico City.

101. Female figurine with feathered headdress, from La Ventilla, Teotihuacán. Terracotta. Museo Nacional de Antropología, Mexico City.

102. Decorative motifs from clay molds created for producing ceramics in series (from Gamio, 1922, Plate 118).

103. Panpipes. Terracotta, height 2 inches. Museo Nacional de Antropología, Mexico City.

104. Warrior dancing, as suggested by footsteps. Atetelco murals, Teotihuacán.

105. Dancing figurine. Terracotta. Museo Nacional de Antropología, Mexico City.

106. Area of recent excavation campaigns in the ceremonial precinct of Teotihuacán.

107. Plan of the Conjunto Habitacional 1E, south of the Templo de Quetzalcoatl in the Ciudadela.
1. Access stairway
2. Central plaza
3. Courtyards of the various sections

108. View of the Conjunto Habitacional 1D from the summit of the Templo de Quetzalcoatl. Note the large central plaza surrounded by residential sections. In the background, the Sun Pyramid.

109. Plan of the Conjunto Habitacional 1C' north of the Templo de Quetzalcoatl in the Ciudadela.
1. Main access
2. Porticoed platform
3. Central courtyard
4. Access stairway to Complex 1D
5. Complex 1D
6. North section of the Gran Plataforma, inside

110. Plan of the Templo de Quetzalcoatl with the later pyramid in front, showing burials and offerings found from 1921 to 1988.
1. Burials found in 1921
2. Offerings found in 1939
3. Burials found during the Proyecto Arqueológico Teotihuacán 1980-82, and in 1983-84

4. Multiple burials explored in 1985
5. Burials explored during the Proyecto Templo de Quetzalcoatl 1988
6. Stratigraphic bores made by the Proyecto Templo de Quetzalcoatl 1988
7. Tunnel

111. Two possible reconstructions of the Templo de Quetzalcoatl. The one on the left proposes six stepped sections (from Marquina, 1951), and the one on the right seven, as suggested by the Proyecto Arqueológico Teotihuacán (from Cabrera and Sugiyama, 1980-82).

112. Multiple burial with nine human skeletons found on the east side of the Templo de Quetzalcoatl.

113. 114. Details of skeletons 6B and 5D found in the burials on the east side of the Templo de Quetzalcoatl. The arms linked behind their backs,

and hands joined as if bound, suggest these are bodies of sacrificial victims.

115. Serpent head with forked tongue. Stairway of the West Plaza Complex, Avenue of the Dead, earlier construction phase (see Plate 99).

116. Jaguar head. Stairway of the West Plaza Complex, Avenue of the Dead, later construction phase (see Plate 98).

117. Teotihuacán mask in serpentine, a stone found in the state of Guerrero. Height 6½ inches.

118. Pipe. Clay, height 2 inches.

119. Molds and clay reproductions found in a workshop of high quality pottery, Cuadrángulo Norte of the Ciudadela.

120. Disk or seal in San Martín Orange Ware, bearing the image of Tlaloc with other symbolic motifs.

Illustration Credits

Plates

Editoriale Jaca Book, Milan (photo Elio Ciol): 31, 37, 38, 40, 74, 80, 83, 85, 89, 90, 91, 92, 93; (photo Antonio Maffeis): 1, 2, 4, 5, 6, 7, 8, 9, 10, 11, 12, 13, 14, 15, 16, 17, 18, 19, 20, 21, 22, 23, 29, 41, 42, 44, 45, 46, 47, 48, 49, 51, 52, 54, 72, 73, 75, 76, 77, 81, 82, 84, 86, 87, 88; (photo Alberto Siliotti): 53, 56, 58, 59, 64, 67, 70, 78, 79.

Instituto Nacional de Antropología e Historia, and Museo Nacional de Antropología, Mexico City: 55, 57, 62, 65, 69, 94, 95, 96, 97, 98, 99, 100, 101, 102, 103, 104, 105, 106, 107, 108, 109; (photo Salvador Guilliem): 27, 28, 60, 61, 63, 66, 68, 71; (photo José de los Reyes): 24, 25, 26, 30, 32, 33, 34, 35, 36, 39.

Luisa Ribolzi, Milan 3, 43, 50.

Illustrations in Text

Photographs

Editoriale Jaca Book, Milan (photo Elio Ciol): 73, 98; (photo Antonio Maffeis): 86.

Instituto Nacional de Antropología e Historia, and Museo Nacional de Antropología, Mexico City: 87, 108, 113, 114, 115, 116, 117, 118, 119, 120; (photo Salvador Guilliem): 85; (photo José de los Reyes): 21, 39, 74, 75, 79, 93, 94, 95, 99, 103.

Rafael Donis, Mexico City: 47.

Line Drawings

Editoriale Jaca Book, Milan (Daniela Balloni): 16, 17, 35, 38, 42, 43, 45; (Enrica Fazzini): 10, 18, 23, 27, 29, 31, 32, 33, 40, 41, 48, 49, 50, 51, 54, 60, 82, 102, 106, 107, 109, 110, 111b; (Fabio Jacomelli): 5, 6, 24, 56, 57, 58, 61, 62, 63, 64, 66, 68, 69, 71, 76, 78, 83, 84, 88, 89, 90, 91, 96, 97, 100, 101, 105.

Instituto Nacional de Antropología e Historia, Mexico City: 26, 30, 34, 36, 37, 46, 52, 55, 59, 104, 112.